P3

Perfect Pocket Planner

A Wedding Planner for brides, written by a bride

Consolidated

By Celina Willone Stewart

©2015 Perfect Pocket Planner
P3 Wedding System, PO Box 1435,
Washington, DC 20013

Photographs generously supplied by **Haese Photography**, 749 Evans
St, Oshkosh, WI 54901. For more information,
visit haesephotography.com or call (920) 243-8330.
Unmarked photos are licensed via Folio.com

Cover & Interior Book Design by **Scribe Freelance**
www.scribefreelance.com

ISBN: 978-09984755-0-9 (Paperback)
ISBN: 0-9760640-5-7 (Binder)
Library of Congress Control Number: 2016921221

To order, visit perfectpocketplanner.com

From water to wine, from pain to love—the road to finding oneself and love is simply the determination to seek what makes you feel whole, loved, and supported. Seek these things at all times, and the aptitude to love and attract love is exponentially increased.

This book is dedicated to all the brides who have begun the beautiful journey towards everlasting love.

Table of Contents

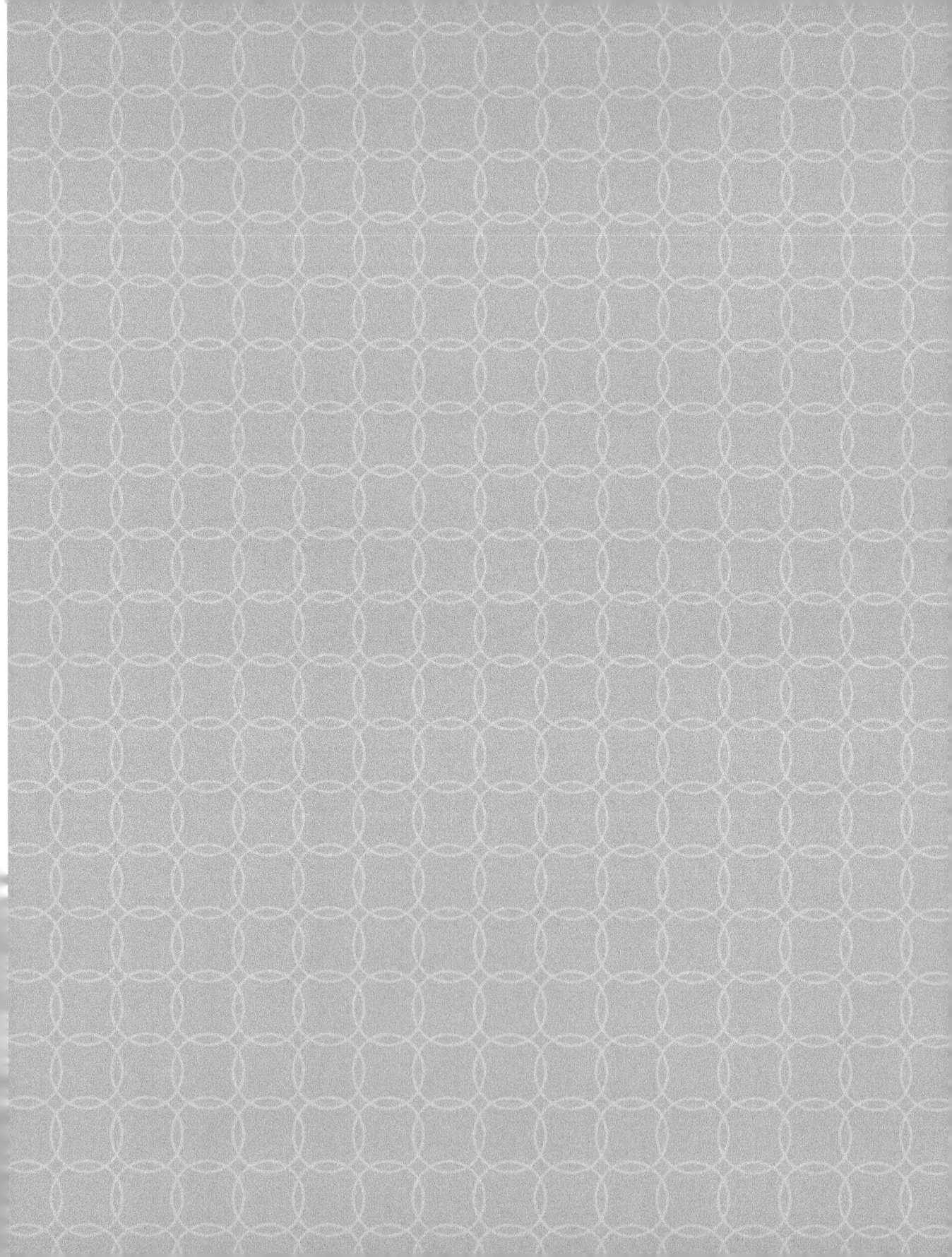

What is the *Perfect Pocket Planner (P3)* All About?

Congratulations on your engagement! You've already made a very wise decision, my friend—determining how you will keep everything organized as you plan your big day. I'm proud of you and thanks for using the P3 system to help you plan one of the most important days of your life.

As a general rule of thumb, you will be saving quite a bit of information between now and the big day. I have found that most items you will keep track of will include receipts, contracts, material swatches, a calendar with appointments, and business cards, just to name a few. This book is the only book on the market written for brides by a recent bride and based 100% on what I needed and created for myself while planning my wedding. I am confident that it will be a huge time saver and stress reliever for you too.

Speaking of saving items let me share with you how this wedding planner got started. When I first became engaged, I knew that I wanted to do the bulk of the planning myself. Knowing that, I set out to find a wedding planner to assist me in keeping everything organized. Thus, the whole reason the P3 book came into existence was because I could not find exactly what I needed in a single planner so I ended up purchasing the two wedding planners that met most of my needs and added the remaining elements I wanted from my local craft store. Part of the reason for my dissatisfaction was that I am an aesthetic person. I like things pretty with clean lines, so I had to take all the stuff from three sources and morph it into my ultimate planner. Changing the book, adding photos of my beloved and me, and adding color tabs—all those additions were my personal style incorporated into this homemade wedding planner. I carried the planner with me *everywhere*! To work, in my weekend bag when I was going places or to any outing, bridal shops, etc. So be sure to carry your book everywhere YOU go so that you never miss out on an opportunity to share your wedding vision when it matters most. When you carry it with you, you never are far away from your wedding vision and trust that by the time you start pulling things together and adding your ideas, you will really start to visualize your ultimate wedding.

HAESE
Photography

The more planning I did the more full my homemade book became. Brides I met in stores noticed my concoction and asked where I purchased it. Honestly, I could not believe people thought my wedding book looked professional enough that I had purchased it somewhere. I was quite smitten with that! After receiving so many inquiries about my book—including requests to recreate the book for other brides—I knew that I had to share this organization tool. It also helped me realize that other brides felt there was more to be had too!

That is why I am thrilled to bring the P3 system to you. Many of my budget brides asked for a consolidated version of my book and here it is. This paperback version is all the text you need and gives you the freedom to create your own book to hold all of your wedding ideas. I made one myself and you can too.

You will find that this wedding planner is a toolkit filled with personal accounts of my own experience where I think it might be helpful but also plenty of tips to help you at each stage of the planning process. As an example, when I was planning it was helpful to know that certain mishaps happened to most brides. Also, when I got engaged the first thing I did (after saying yes, doing the happy dance and sharing the news with my closest family and friends) was figure out how to plan an amazing event filled with amazing food and an experience that we would enjoy and our guests would remember for years to come. I share details that I believe many wedding planners and brides do not always openly share—from handling family drama to overcoming headaches that come along with working with new vendors.

Now let's get started. Cheers!

CHAPTER 1: *Budget*

Well, here we are! If you have this planner, you are probably recently engaged and planning your wedding. By now I am sure you have read all about weddings and all the beauty of this momentous occasion. Hold on to those warm and fuzzies, but now it is time to get to business!

Wondering why I'm spoiling all the fun of planning your wedding by talking about money right out the gate? Let me tell you: this item is the single most important starting part of the wedding. Unless you just have oodles of money or an unlimited budget you will need to determine the amount up front you can spend before you do any planning. And if you do have an unlimited budget, you will still need a way to keep yourself organized.

If you remember nothing else keep this image in your head, where the money flows (pun intended) is how the wedding goes. In other words, think of *your wedding as a boat and your budget as the water that the wedding floats upon.*

In this section, I will show you how to breakdown your budget, how to effectively stay on budget, and how to make adjustments once you begin securing vendors. Lets begin with determining your budget amount.

Preliminary Budget Research

When I started my wedding planning I thought asking a bride or her parents what they paid for the wedding was like asking a person how much money they earn or what kind of car they drive, but it is not! Brides are usually really open about how much they spent and the value of what they paid. If you find that someone is not willing to share how much he or she spent on elements of the wedding, it is usually because the wedding was a bit exorbitant. So go ahead and ask!

While researching wedding costs, there are many reliable sources such as popular wedding websites and the local wedding magazines. Talking to newlyweds, a reputable wedding consultant, and even reviewing wedding statistics online can also be valuable. But ultimately, your budget should be based on what is most feasible and comfortable for *you*.

I looked online for typical wedding costs and found reviews online. My own budget was below the average but I was determined to keep my wedding budget intact. So what was a girl to do? Be resourceful!

I took a somewhat unconventional approach to determine if my budget was wildly below market. Many brides determine how much money they have, divvy up the budget by percentages and start looking for vendors that are within budget. Instead of doing this, I started reaching out to vendors to get quotes.

As a natural problem solver I did the only thing that made sense: I found a solid wedding planner with tons of resources and we started gathering information. We met with no less than 3 vendors per category and got prices to see the high and low ranges in the area. For example, I live in a large metropolitan area that is flanked by several suburbs. In my area the average wedding in the city was $45,000. In the neighboring suburbs the average was around $30,000 - $35,000. My budget was $25,000. Thus, if you have a set budget that is competitive with other weddings in your area, you may not need to do what I did. However, if your situation is anything like mine then reaching out for vendor quotes could be the best way to determine what your budget can yield and whether what you have in mind is truly realistic. For me reaching out made planning and securing my vendors quick and easy, especially after getting the big picture on costs I was able to see where I could to spend a little more money and where I could save money. I am even including a copy of my own budget as a sample so you can see how I did it in Chapter 15: *Resources.*

In the end, I was able to afford exactly the wedding I wanted without sacrificing quality and style. This system worked fabulously for me! I say that to let you know, whether you have below market budget or an over the top budget, you can have the wedding you want if you follow the tips in this book and are willing to think outside the box to get what you need. You are likely to end up with the best day you have ever created!

Wedding Contributors

Even if you know exactly what you want your parents may hold the purse strings for your big day. Now, this can be a touchy topic ladies so buckle up. Traditionally, the bride's parents pay for the bulk of the wedding expenses. How that bulk is divided really depends on the family. Perhaps the bride's parents are taking the traditional approach and paying for everything or perhaps the bride and groom and bride's parents are splitting the cost 50/50. Or maybe your grandparents, aunts/uncles or other family members are all giving a donation. Ultimately, it can get confusing determining who will have a say about what in a situation where someone else's money is involved in your wedding. So, how much say will your parents or other contributors have?

If you and your parents always agree, splendid! But the likelihood of that is really rare, so you will have to be really be conscientious if situations begin to arise. I would suggest that you just have a conversation with the contributors in the beginning. You should discuss your vision for the wedding, thank them for the money they are contributing and ask them what parts of the wedding are most important to them as far as participation. Maybe they just want to make sure the food is appropriate for the generational guests or want to make sure the venue is convenient. Find out in the beginning so that you can avoid any issues during the planning process. You will be thanking your lucky stars if you are able to handle this before the money comes rolling in. I would even consider writing down the result of the conversation so that you do not forget to include them in parts that are important. As you get closer to the wedding, there are so many details, and unless you are keeping good track, things can get lost.

If you and your groom are paying for the wedding you can avoid these conversations altogether. My guess is even if you are, your parents and loved ones may still want to have some input. Nonetheless, things have really evolved as far as who contributes to a wedding, so it is good to have a frame of reference. Below is a traditional breakdown of how wedding costs are assigned:

Bride and/or Bride's Parents
- Grooms wedding ring and gift
- Invitations, reception cards and announcements
- Wedding gown and accessories
- Fee for ceremony location
- Décor and flowers for ceremony and reception
- Photography & music
- Reception (venue, food, activities)

Groom and/or Groom's Parents
- Brides wedding ring and engagement ring
- Gift for bride
- Marriage license
- Minister, pastor or officiates fee
- Brides bouquet & mothers corsages, boutonnieres for groomsmen
- Rehearsal dinner
- Honeymoon
- Groomsmen lodging (optional)

Budget Breakdown: Default Scenario[1]

Ok, so we know there is a lot to do but you may be unsure as to how to appropriate your money. Just know that your budget will change based on who is contributing money for your wedding. But, what percentage goes towards the reception, your dress, flowers and all the other things that make up a wedding? Well, let's start by determining what amounts typically are allocated for what. The example is based on my own $25,000 budget.

Expense Category $25,000	Budget %	Budget $
Reception, catering & venue	50%	$12,500
Ceremony	3%	$750
Flowers & Décor	10%	$2,500
Photography/ Videography	8%	$2,000
Wedding Attire	10%	$2,500
Rentals	1%	$250

[1] Be advised that wedding sources differ on how to allocate the budget. While these values worked best for me, you should adjust your percentages to reflect your wedding priorities. This should be used as a guide.

Music & Lighting	8%	$2,000
Guest Correspondence (invitations, etc.)	5%	$1250
Transportation	3%	$750
Gifts	2%	$500
TOTAL	**100%**	**$25,000**

How the Internet can help your budget

A proactive way to save money in the budget is through applying for online wedding offers. Online contests are everywhere so create a wedding email account early (read: now) and sign up for as many websites as you can. You can win everything from party favors, wedding and bridesmaid dresses, photography packages, bridal showers, honeymoons and even a whole wedding. A few weeks after the wedding you can delete or deactivate the email account if you wish and not have to worry about getting endless emails anymore. Again, I advise signing up for these websites sooner rather than later. Many contest winners have a year to spend the prize money so unless you are planning a long engagement you should be able to use much of it for your own wedding and pre-wedding parties. You may even be able to use it for a first post-wedding party. Also, take a peek to see if there are restrictions on when and how you can use the prize money. Chances are, the rules will be flexible enough for your big day but just double check.

Saving On Those Extra Things

Unless there is another really important reason for having your wedding date on everything, do not date stamp your wedding napkins. If you omit the date, you can use those favors for later parties that you and your future husband host. It will still be a nice touch and also will help make your dollar go further in the long run.

Wait to purchase the ring bearers pillow, cake servers or toasting glasses. You use them once and then you will rarely use them again. However, if you have extra money left over in your budget closer to the wedding and you still want them you can purchase them at that time.

Make your favors or attendant's gifts if you are crafty.

Buy things as you have the cash for them. For example, if money is an issue purchase stamps for your Save-the-Dates separate from the stamps you will need for your wedding invitation and response cards. If you do this just make sure that the post office will have the stamps you need year round. Special occasion stamps are often times unavailable or sold out by the time you need them. Also, ask the cashier about wedding, engagement or party stamps. When I was stamp shopping, I learned that there was a great selection of wedding stamps to choose from and it created a seamless look from the Save-the-Dates to the wedding invitation and response cards. You can visit your local post office to view stamps or visit _www.usps.com_ to see what is available online. I recommend going to the post office because often times the stock online differs from what the local post office may carry.

Cutting your wedding costs is very feasible. Another tip I suggest is checking out wedding magazines and websites for articles on saving costs. Trust me, there are tons of wedding books about how to save money. Some of the ideas really resonated with me. It may be that way for you as well. My advice is read the books about saving wedding dollars; keep track of the ideas and jot them down in this book or in your phone. I found that my local library had a really great selection of wedding books. I encourage you to check out your local library to see what they have on hand as well. If you do you will walk away with knowledge about some pretty smart ways to save some cash!

Calculating a Consultant Fee into the Budget

If you are including the consultant in your overall budget the above percentages will have to be adjusted. Fees for wedding consultants vary across the board. Some planner fees are a percentage of the overall budget while others have a standard fee based on size of wedding or amount of work. Either way, it could add up to a hefty penny. As for me, I paid for my consultant out of my savings and I kept her fee totally separate from the wedding budget. If your consultant's fee is a part of the budget, ask her to draw up a new budget with her fee included. They should be able to do this pretty quickly for you. They will be pretty motivated since they want to get paid as well. If your consultant fees will be paid out of the overall budget, deduct that amount and then use the remaining balance as your working budget. The following example shows how a $25,000 budget will be adjusted to include a wedding consultant who charges 20% of total budget.

Expense Category Budget= $25,000	Budget %	Budget $
Bridal Consultant Fee	20%	$5000
Working Wedding Budget		$20,000
Reception, catering & venue	50%	$10,000
Ceremony	3%	$600
Flowers & Décor	10%	$2,000
Photography/ Videography	8%	$1,600
Wedding Attire	10%	$2,000
Rentals	1%	$200
Music & Lighting	8%	$1,600
Guest Correspondence (invitations, etc.)	5%	$1000
Transportation	3%	$600
Gifts	2%	$400
TOTAL	100%	$25,000

Finding a Bridal Consultant

While we are on the topic of finding a great consultant, if you know a wedding consultant you trust...AWESOME! But if you are like me and need recommendations, here are some tips to help you narrow down the right consultant for you. Fortunately, finding a consultant in today's market it is much simpler than it was for our mother's generation. Nowadays, you can find someone wonderful with just a click of a button. Or if you have friends or family members who have recently wed in your area, you can always ask about their experience and get real time feedback on the consultant. I used a few different methods to scout for my consultant, including doing Internet searches, asking friends and family, and also meeting with consultants at wedding shows. Ultimately, I decided on a phenomenal lady who my own mother recommended. My consultant had been part of the wedding industry for almost a decade as an assistant and was ready to strike out on her own. Because she'd never planned a wedding from beginning to end, she gave us a discount for her services and resources in exchange for a glowing recommendation and pictures to use for her website. I also agreed to help draft her services contract so everyone was happy all around. It was a bit of luck and a blessing that she turned out to be pretty amazing and the perfect personality to help plan my wedding. The takeaway: be open and the universe will likely conspire to get you what you need.

Ok, so first things first: decide if you need a part time or a full time consultant. A part time consultant can basically be like a wedding assistant—you do much of the decision-making and they will assist you with whatever planning you need and can offer vendors in your area that they have worked with.

A full-time consultant usually will talk to you about your vision and they do all the planning for you. You can have as much or as little say as you want throughout the process and they will do all the heavy lifting such as setting up appointments and following up with each vendor during the process.

Most consultants have fun little names for the different packages they offer and each package outlines what is included in the price so pay attention, do some comparison shopping and make sure that you and the consultant get along prior to signing any contract. The last thing you want is a control freak wanting to create their dream wedding and not yours, or someone who you really do not like planning your special day. This seems so basic and a no-brainer but you would be surprised.

P3 Tips For Finding A Bridal Consultant

- Someone who has planned at least a dozen weddings will bring the necessary experience to get the job done.
- Interview several consultants and go with the person you feel most comfortable with and who clearly understands your wedding vision.
- Get referrals from family and friends, recent brides or meet with consultants at bridal expos.
- Ask another planner whose work you respect for recommendations if they are unavailable or out of your price range.
- Check yellow pages, Internet, bridal sites and review sites.
- Contact the Association of Bridal Consultants in your area for recommendations (https://www.bridalassn.com).

Checking Your Bridal Consultant's Work

One way to know if your consultant is up to snuff is if they are registered member of a bridal organization or bridal trade organizations. Whether the consultant is registered or not you will want to get references and check reviews. When collecting references be sure to get the phone number if possible for specific questions.

A quick note about references: when you ask for references obviously your planner will give you names and numbers of some of their best clients. I strongly suggest talking with them over the phone. You definitely do not want to come across as pessimistic or looking for drama but you want to know the real deal about the planner. Here are a few questions that I asked:

1. How long ago was your event?
2. Did planner and staff arrive on time?
3. Was planner with you from beginning to end? If not, when did he/she arrive?
4. How available was planner for last minute meetings or changes?
5. What did you enjoy most about your wedding?
6. Did he/she produce your dream wedding or come close?
7. If planner could improve upon one thing, what would it be?

Adjusting Your Budget As Vendors Are Secured

I highly recommend updating your budget whenever a change occurs. That means when you secure a vendor, if you cancel or add something, and all other adjustments which impact the budget, no matter how small the change seems. This is really the only way to stay on top of everything. Please believe me when I tell you that you will literally deal with multiple people a day as you begin to plan so recording the changes on the budget will ensure that nothing is missed.

Using the sample budget including the bridal consultant's fee lets say that you find a venue that is $4,000 and the food and beverage total another $5000. That means that you have spent $9000, leaving you with $1000 remaining. You will want to keep track of that as you continue to plan so that you know exactly how much money you are working with in each category. Furthermore, you can re-allocate money in areas where there is extra to fund those areas that may be slightly over budget. You should keep these numbers clear so that you do not end up in a situation where you have blown your budget without knowing it. Any extra money can also be used to purchase those last minute items like the ring bearer pillow discussed earlier. The budget resources in Chapter 15 can certainly help you stay on track.

CHAPTER 2: *Contract Basics*

Now, I know a little something about contracts since I have done many of them in my field of work. This is an important logistical skill and I would not be me if I did *not highly* encourage you to double cross your t's and dot your i's. But I am going to make it really simple for you and give you a quick and dirty recap of my two cents on the process. This is not legal advice but simply me sharing what helped me during the planning process on this front.

The parts of a contract are pretty straightforward but states can vary on how it is defined so be sure to look up your local laws for any specifics on this basic definition. A contract usually consists of three parts: (1) Offer of goods and/or services; (2) Acceptance of the terms; and (3) Consideration. This is the very lofty way of outlining so I will break it down to real people terms.

The Offer

A contract is nothing more than an outline of the terms and responsibilities of the parties contracting. Specifically, an offer is between the buyer (you) and seller (vendor—i.e. baker and DJ). When you are dealing with businesses, they will almost always have a contract outlining their services. Most of these contracts are pretty standard and are based upon important things like the state laws and regulations. Be sure to read all contracts that you are given and have your wedding consultant or someone you trust review them as well. The standard terms are usually not the issue. What becomes the issue are any specific items that the business will offer based on your individualized needs. So just know that because weddings are so personal, most standardized contracts will not totally hit the mark every time. Make sure there are no red flags in the standard language and that the services or goods that the vendor is providing are in writing.

Acceptance

Acceptance is as simple as both parties agreeing to the terms of a contract and signed by you and the vendor. Review every line of the contract to be sure that what you want is included. Once you are comfortable with the terms, go ahead and sign on the dotted line baby doll! Oh, and make sure that both you and the vendor have a copy with both your and the vendor's signatures. When both parties have signed, the document has been "executed" and becomes the official agreement between you and each vendor.

Consideration

This simply means an exchange, which the parties have relied upon. In these types of situations you are offering money in exchange for the vendor producing goods or services. You paid money with the expectation that the vendor will provide the agreed upon services. This type of transaction is no different than shopping and paying for your purchase in a store, but now you just have a fancy way to describe the transaction.

P3 Tips for Contracts

- Take your time to read each contract. Never sign a contract in the moment unless it was sent to you before hand and you have already viewed it. If you do not understand or like a term, ask about it or request for a change. You normally have at least a day or so to look it over and "sleep" on it so to speak.
- Put down as little as possible (10-25%). **Never** put more than 50% down on anything.
- Be vigilant against large cancellation fees. Last minute cancellation fees are to be expected but you should not have to pay the bulk of cost if you cancel well in advance (e.g. 3-6 months is usually reasonable but read the contract and see how the vendor outlines cancellation fees.) If by chance cancellation fees are not included ask about it and get it added to the contract.
- If any vendor refuses to sign a contract then that is a huge red flag. All I can say is if you find it difficult to get the contract back signed simply move on.
- Consider buying wedding insurance. You can find reputable wedding insurance carriers by doing a simple search online for "wedding insurance in [your city, state]" and you are likely to get a list of several. If you are having a wedding at home then ask your home insurer, to see what may be covered. I'll discuss this more in the following paragraphs.

The Wedding Dress Contract

While shopping for my dress the dressmaker who was also the owner-designer wanted me to pay for the dress in full prior to any measurements being done and before I could even see or try on the dress. Though I thought she was brilliant and fun, I walked right out of there and found my dress elsewhere. I did so because once you've paid for any item in full there is less incentive to give you stellar customer service. I know better than that and now you do too.

Here are a few additional tips to help you:

- Expect the down payment to be anywhere from 10 to 50 percent of costs. If the shop requires full payment beware and find another shop.
- Balance and due dates for payments should be outlined.
- Detailed description of dress including starting measurements of bust, waist, hips and length of gown.
- Each required alteration and associate cost is described in full detail including the upcoming fitting dates or deadlines.
- The promised delivery date is stated in contract.
- A cancellation provision, specifying that the deposit will be refunded if the clothing doesn't arrive in the desired condition or at the very least reasonably good condition.

A friend of mine shared an unfortunate situation that occurred while shopping for her daughter's wedding dress. The dress was a ribbon dress with extensive detailing. The dress was supposed to flatter figures such as the bride. However, when the dress arrived at the shop, the ribbons were disjointed and the length of the dress was at least 2 inches too short for the bride. It was obvious that the ribbon detail was severely compromised. My friend had to really push to get the maker to correct the mistakes and had notes of exactly the information exchanged. In the end, she ended up paying several hundreds of dollars for extra fittings, which was a big headache! Moral of he story is find out what these fees are in advance in case mistakes occur.

Wedding Insurance

Just as you insure your vehicle or the belongings in your home, you can also insure certain accidents that occur before and during your wedding. You should count on coverage costing about 2 percent of your overall wedding budget. Some brides opt to go without insurance, which is up to you, but having wedding insurance does provide a layer of protection. Here are some features and benefits that are typically included:

Cancellation and postponement provision: while this will not cover a change of heart, there is coverage for an unforeseen delay based on natural disasters or other factors that are otherwise out of your control. Check the fine print for what qualifies for coverage under this provision.

Liability Coverage: unfortunate accidents could occur at your wedding, for example—a guest being injured during the ceremony or reception. Should something happen and the facility is not responsible for the accident, your insurance likely will cover those expenses. You will want to check the policy for any exclusion that may apply. It will be spelled out in the policy so just be sure to pay attention and read the policy carefully.

Covered Events: this is an important provision because it will outline which events during the wedding weekend are covered. The rehearsal dinner, the ceremony and reception are commonly covered but depending on the insurer there may be more events covered. If the policy covers more than those three that is a huge bonus that you should take advantage of.

Determining your wedding theme is very important, as it likely will guide the food you serve, the venue you choose, the wedding attire and the decorations. From the moment your guests arrive at the ceremony and reception it should be clear what the style or theme is, and that theme should reflect you and the groom. Since weddings are so personal, it is really the first time guests will have the opportunity to see a couple's style. This was really important to me so we wanted to make sure that we tended to every detail to ensure that guests understood who we were as a couple and it was fun to plan.

For example, if both you and your fiancé are from Boston and love baseball, you could easily turn that into a theme by having Boston favorites on the menu and using the team colors as your wedding colors. Think outside the box. No need to be so stringent by having baseballs (unless you want to), instead do what makes sense to you and is fun. The idea would be to just give folks the feel of Boston and the things that matter most to you as a couple.

One of the first questions I asked was: how in the world do I simplify all that my beloved and me are in a single theme? It was a bit overwhelming but it did force me to really think about the relationship and the things that were important to us. Lucky for you, this is covered this in Chapter 5 on Venue. But if you are still unsure, another easy way to see tons of wedding ideas in a single space is to attend local bridal shows. The worksheet in Chapter 15 will also help you.

Bridal Shows

Even though I eventually decided to hire a wedding planner, I still regularly attended bridal shows and it was one of our favorite parts of planning. Wedding shows are announced in the paper, on wedding websites, and even bridal shops. In addition, once you attend one bridal expo, you will be added to a list and get emails from the bridal show organizers. Attending these bridal expos is also a great way to get familiar with vendors in the area so I highly recommend attending a few or as many as you can stand. Do not be shy about talking to these folks about what you want or envision for your wedding. I found that I really enjoyed going to see, taste, smell and feel everything. The brides in attendance also seem to have taken the happy pill so it is an amazing energizer for getting pumped up about your own wedding.

Oh, and did I mention that most shows have door prizes?! The door prizes are not too shabby either. Many of the shows had giveaways for honeymoons, wedding ring sets, free makeup on your wedding day, winning a planner for your wedding, and full photography packages just to name a few. There were also cash prizes. If you are not the lucky winner at a show just know that the more shows you attend the greater your chance of winning. Even if you do not ever win the bigger prizes, the loot bag that you get at each show is usually AMAZING! The vendors will bring samples of their product so from nearly every show we walked away with cookie and cake samples, pens, cards, gadgets, cookware, utensils, candy, and so much more! Now, my fiancé was crazy about these bags and was not one bit shy about grabbing everything in sight (I am the more modest one if you can imagine). This man would leave with bags filled with all types of goodies and I thought he would go insane from glee. Fortunately for me, we only needed to attend 5 shows before I had all the vendors secured so I was spared any further embarrassment.

So again, unless you know exactly what you want already and even if you do go to the shows! Have a great time enjoying all things wedding because once the wedding is over you probably will not have an opportunity to enjoy anything like this smorgasbord again.

Check Your Expectations

You will find there are one-stop shops you can visit that will do it all: from the DJ to décor. That setup did not work for me because I found that no one company does everything exceptionally well but that doesn't mean it is not out there. The fact that I am also super picky probably did not help matters. Nonetheless, I know many brides who were able to find one stop shops who met their needs perfectly and they had fabulous weddings with a lot less stress since they only had to deal with one company. There are certainly perks!

HAESE
Photography

When you do attend bridal shows, also check out how booths are set up. Often times it will give you ideas about your own wedding or help you narrow down a style. It can also show you what you do not want as well. Either way, it provides valuable information on the vendor's organizational capabilities and provides a lot of ideas on what is currently popular. I suggest taking pictures of anything that you love during these shows. Even if you do not ever think you will use the ideas, they often come in handy somewhere down the line somehow. Keep it in your back pocket of ideas.

P3 Tips for Getting the Most From Bridal Shows

Bridal shows present a unique opportunity for brides. It is a single location where you can find a plethora of talented vendors in one place. Thus, when you go, here is how you can get the most out of these shows.

– Talk to the people behind the booths
– Consider the following: Are products something you would like to have for a part of your wedding? Are vendors personable? Is the company customer service oriented?
– Pick up the brochures and handouts available and make note of what you like. It's a great starting point.

Holiday Themed Weddings

I also want to add a quick note if you are having your wedding on a holiday. To that end, themed weddings can be really fun and make décor a breeze since most venues are decked out for holidays like Halloween, Christmas, or New Year's.

In my city it was difficult to find the exact date we wanted. While scouting venues one of staffers asked if getting married during Christmas or New Year's was an option. She showed me pictures of the venue all decked out in holiday lights and it was beautiful. It got me thinking about how getting married during this time was not only cheaper because December is an off-peak time but a bride could also save money since the venue would already be decorated! That was a really great tip that could be helpful to you.

It's probably obvious not how much savings you will have if the venue is already decorated, and you should consider that option if a particular holiday is significant or if you have a tight budget. Depending on the weather, location, and durability of your guests, this could be the decision that keeps that budget intact.

CHAPTER 4: *Wardrobe*

What the bride and groom wear is very memorable for guests. Thus, nail the look on your big day and people will be talking about it for ages. There is much covered in this chapter, so it is helpful to give a roadmap. Since menswear and the bridal attendant attire are both pretty straightforward, we will start with those sections. The remaining sections are all about the bridal gown. The sections below are full of helpful information from the time you step foot in a salon and the fittings up to the day of the wedding. Here we go!

Wedding Formalities

The level of formality will dictate the types of formalwear your bridal party will wear. In general, there are four types of wedding formalities. When I started planning, I did not realize that the size of your wedding coincides with how snazzy the event will be. If this is news to you as well, I will share with you how this conundrum works. Feel free to totally defy tradition if you want but here are the guideposts.

How formal is your wedding?

Very formal:	200+ guests
Formal:	150+ guests
Semi-formal:	100 guests or less
Informal:	50 guests or less

Menswear

If you are anything like me, you may not be well versed in men's attire. To be quite honest, I was not interested in delving too deeply into the process of finding out. This is where your groom will come in handy. Before the groomsmen attend their fittings, the groom will have decided the style and color of his digs for the day. That will guide what the groomsmen wear. Usually, they wear the same style suit with a boutonniere or matching tie. All in all, I just wanted to know the basics and have an idea of what the men would wear so I could visualize. So whether you are a fashionista with extensive knowledge of men's formal wear or a novice like me, I am here to bring you up to speed. Fortunately, there are only a few categories for you to know in order to get the job done:

Semi-formal evening
Formal suit or jacket with matching trousers, white shirt, cummerbund, black bow tie, studs and cufflinks; and

Formal evening
Black dinner jacket and trousers, white tuxedo shirt, waistcoat, black 4 in hand tie, cummerbund or vest, and cufflinks.

Ordering the Tuxes

Not only do the groom and groomsman suits coordinate but their suits should also blend with bridesmaid dresses as well. One sure way to brighten up a tuxedo and blend the overall theme is by having groomsmen wear accessories such as vests, ties or bow ties that match or complement the bridesmaid dresses. For my own wedding I planned for my bridesmaids to wear a deep grape colored dress and had planned for the groom to wear a rainbow tie with grape accents. We decided the groomsmen would look nice in ties that were died to match the color of the bridesmaid's dresses. You can do something similar in your own wedding.

As a final note, ask the formalwear shop about exact prices, including alterations and inquire about the return policy or deadlines for returning the suits or tuxedos. When you are attending wedding shows be sure to visit the menswear booths, which usually have great deals. One of the most popular deals is one where the groom gets his tuxedo free after a certain number of suits or tuxes are rented. Usually the requirement is a do-able number—like 3 or 4 rentals. If it is more than that try including the fathers of the bride and groom suits', the ring bearer and ushers suits. This ensures you get a great discount and also makes it more likely that all the suits are the same style and color. It also makes returning easy since if all the suits can be returned to the same shop or retailer.

HAESE
Photography

Your Attendant's Attire

When you are planning your own wedding for the first time it is easy to lose sight of the whole picture. P3 is here to help you avoid that mistake in your own preparation. It was helpful for me to sketch out what folks were wearing from a group photograph

perspective. Another suggestion would be looking at as many wedding photos as you can. You can visit local photographer websites which usually have galleries online for you to view free of charge.

Typically, bridesmaids wear identical dresses while the honor attendant wears something slightly different. Here are a few variations you might consider:

- Choose dresses in the same color and fabric but let your girls style it differently. There are now convertible dresses that transition to a halter, one shoulder, strapless, and a few other necklines. The fabric is usually a stretch fabric so if this appeals to you ask whomever you work with at the bridal or dress shop. They should be able to show you the different fabrics and different ways to wear the dresses. With so many options, your bridesmaids will be thrilled to implement their own style during your wedding.
- Select a single dress but allow bridesmaids to wear coordinating colors for your wedding. Most dresses come in an array of colors. If you choose this option just be sure to see the colors on the girls and be sure to take pictures so that your florist can coordinate other parts of your wedding as one fluid experience.
- Include printed dresses into the mix. I was terrified of including patterns and prints into bridesmaid dresses but I had a more classic vibe. However, if you have a safari theme, prints could work fabulously. My only advice is get pictures and a second opinion of someone whose style you trust. I have seen several ethnic weddings, which included beautiful cloths that made the wedding feel very festive. I encourage you to look at it all together. The goal is to ensure that what you want is represented while avoiding your wedding turning into a costume party.

It is time to decide what your bridesmaids will wear. As I mentioned above, be sure to see the whole picture. During the wedding you will be so busy enjoying the moment, greeting folks, dancing, and laughing but just remember your guests are seeing it all come together so the dresses should fit with your theme in terms of design and color. As long as you try to coordinate the dresses, flowers, cake, and decor you will be on the right path to having a seamless color palette. Some of the best places to go for gorgeous gowns are bridal shops but you can also find some great options at department stores. I was really intent on avoiding a large-scale retailer for my wedding gown and bridesmaid dresses because I wanted something more unique. But after shopping at several dress shops, I found the bridesmaid dresses at a retailer. And it looked fabulous on all the ladies. I am not sure about your girlfriends but mine are pretty different in size and height. It was nothing short of a miracle that I found something I loved and that they loved wearing.

There is another logistical matter I want to address. When planning my own wedding, my bridesmaids were in different parts of the country so I chose a national manufacturer for their dresses so that alterations could be done easily and at their convenience. But it can be just as easy if you have the dresses made by a good seamstress. The seamstress will measure the girls and the dresses will be customized to fit them. Then the dresses can either be sent to them in advance for final alternations at a local shop or the girls just come in for a final fitting and alterations the week of the wedding. A good seamstress will be able to turn it around pretty quickly, assuming your bridesmaid's sizes do not change dramatically. One nugget of advice is to make sure you let your bridesmaids know the ideal length so you do not have several different hemlines on your wedding day. So just be sure to let them know how short they can go with alterations to their dresses if it's being done across multiple seamstresses.

The Bridal Gown

Now that you know how formal your affair will be and the budget for your dress, lets talk gowns. I quickly realized that my budget was just below what was standard in my area. No surprise since my budget was below market. Keep in mind your gown and the wedding will depend not only on the style of your wedding but also where you choose to have it. It is also important to know that wedding shops in urban areas tend to be pricier than those in the suburbs or rural areas. So if you truly want something unique at a great price, taking a trip a little further outside of your area may be worth it. This is just something to keep in mind.

What is your style? Initially, I could not speak to all the features in a dress I wanted. It took me a little time and study to determine not only what I liked, but also what worked best for my figure. Then you take that and translate it into a dress within your budget. Whew...bring on the stress, right? Fortunately, bridal salons are filled with talented folks who fit brides for a living or at least enough to give you some pretty solid guidance. However, before you go to the bridal salon try and figure out what you want in the following categories.

Fabric

Consider when you are having your wedding. If you are having a winter wedding you will need a heavier fabric unless you live in a climate that's warm all year round. If you are having a spring or fall wedding you have more flexibility in the fabric because you can go lighter or heavier just depending on what you want. Summer definitely calls for lighter fabrics unless the event is taking place indoors. Whenever the season, if you are having any part of your wedding outside you will have to take into account mother nature and how that might impact your overall comfort during the ceremony and reception.

Sleeve

If you hate having your arms out then sleeves are the way to go. But if you could care less then there are many options both with and without sleeves. By the way, a good dress shop can add or take off sleeves depending on what you want and need.

Length

When I was shopping I saw styles that I never imagined I would love. There are several options including chic knee length dresses, mid-calf to traditional long gowns. Tell your bridal consultant the theme and some details about your wedding and they will help guide you.

Trains

There are three types to consider (1) the sweep: as it sounds it just touches the floor, (2) the chapel length: extends three to four feet behind the gown, and (3) the cathedral: the most extravagant of lengths extends six to eight feet behind the dress.

The Bridal Accessories

These are all the fun things you will wear to coordinate with your gown. When you are in bridal shops try to avoid accessory overload. Here is an illustration of what I mean:

P3 Tip: Overcoming Dress Obstacles

The first dress shop was one I visited year's prior during another wedding I was in. The current reviews were still pretty solid, so I decided to go with the shop I knew. I scheduled an appointment and took all the necessary precautions to ensure the fitting went beautifully, or so I thought. When my bridesmaids and I showed up, the place smelled like a stale sandwich shop and they refused to allow us to use the restrooms. It was positively awful and I was heart broken. It was nothing like it had been when I went years before. Fortunately, I had a fairy godmother of a wedding planner who was able to work us into another shop in no time flat, even on a Saturday.

At the final salon the fitting went much smoother. The owner helped me herself and was able to problem solve all types of issues at every point in the process. It was during this fitting that I realized that the salon helpers are there to completely outfit you. That is awesome if they just happen to pinpoint exactly what type of bride and personality you have. So while the lady was such a dear soul who really knew how to work a dress, she had me in earrings and veils that were way too outdated for someone like me. I considered myself a modern bride and I wanted to look a certain way and you should look the way you want as well. I say all this to tell you speak up! If the earrings look like they would be better suited for your 80-year-old grandmother then just politely take them off and say, "what else do you have?" You could also ask, "do you have something more classic or modern to go with this dress?" Once you get that out, it sends a clear message to the salesperson what you want and that you are vested in finding the right look for you. An effective salesperson that knows her stuff will catch the hint quickly and make the necessary adjustments to secure the sale.

Even if you do not have a wedding planner to save the day, have a back up plan. Bridal shops further off the beaten path may have similar openings even on a Saturday. Another option is to set up two appointments on the same day or in the same weekend. This just means maybe you schedule two Saturday appointments: one in the morning and the other in the late afternoon or one appointment on each day of the weekend. Worse case scenario, you will visit one shop but best-case scenario is you have multiple options to choose from.

When I shopped for my dress I was fortunate to have most of my bridesmaids in attendance for the fitting. You will learn this could be a rarity since friends often times live all across the country. If you are fortunate to have everyone in the same city count yourself lucky because they will back you if your consultant goes a little crazy with the accessories.

Also, feel free to purchase parts of your wedding ensemble form a multiple dress shops or stores. Once I knew the styles that actually worked best, I looked online for the other pieces I needed. However, check the return policy in case what you think your getting turns out to be different than your expectations.

Working for the world's leading lingerie brand for a few years taught me that what a woman wears under her clothes are just as important as the clothes itself. In the following paragraphs I share a list of accessories that you will likely need for your beautiful day and some specific tips on how to best achieve a flawless look.

Lingerie

Once you have your dress the next thing you will want to figure out is your undergarment. No need to purchase all your lingerie from the bridal shop, which can be more expensive. Do try on or have the salesperson show you which undergarments are recommended. If the price is reasonable, great but if not then find what you need elsewhere and call it a day. Try everything on prior to your wedding day to ensure it is the right fit.

Brassiere

I always recommend wearing a bra. How the dress is cut does not matter because there is almost always a bra that can work. And this is coming from someone who worked in the best selling lingerie business for years. It can be less than classy to take photos with your goods showing through the fabric and everyone knows that a camera catches far more than the eye. Why take a risk like that on such an important day?

Slimming accessories

We all have flaws, but some women know it, embrace it and deal with it head on and some do not. If wearing the modern day girdle is absolutely not for you or you are just naturally slim all over, be sure to take a few pictures beforehand to make sure you look the way you want.

Stocking/Hosiery

If your wedding is happening in late spring or summer I would say skip stocking and hosiery and get a great leg waxing. However, if your wedding is in the winter months, hosiery provides warmth and creates a clean line in a dress.

Finally, your accessories should reflect the formality of occasion, season and style of your wedding. When thinking about your jewelry keep in mind that the more ornate the gown, the simpler the jewelry. As you probably know, diamonds and pearls are timeless but you can do more elaborate jewelry if you want. Again, I suggest taking a photo of yourself fully dressed so you can see how everything looks together. As an aside, any handbag should be small and compliment your dress. Most brides do not bother with a handbag until the reception or not at all.

Finding the Best Shape

Working ten years in retail taught me so much about dressing women. From my years in lingerie to clothing I have seen it all—literally. But the most important lesson was that every woman is different and that is a beautiful thing. I learned so much about how to make any woman, regardless of size and shape, look and feel her most fabulous.

Essentially, style is really all about finding the clothes that accentuate the most complimentary parts of your shape and minimizes those areas that are not as flattering. Thus, how you are shaped and what you are comfortable in should always rule the garment choice. Below is an outline of ideas and suggestions for a variety of figures.

Full figured

Choose a long, A-line or simple style and embrace the lighter weight fabrics if they have a good lining or you have a good cincher underneath. Many stylists say stay away from lightweight fabrics and choose a more structured fabric, but I have seen that both work. If you're worried about your arms you can always try a dress with sleeves to make your arms appear smaller and consider a sheer fabric if during the warmer months. Finally, a V-neck and drop waist dress will take the emphasis off hips and can accentuate the bust line. You should also consider diagonal pleated gowns.

Petite

Avoid exaggerated details. Look for dresses that give the appearance of you being taller or elongates your waist, legs or neck. Think a sheath or princess lined gown. Make sure that any embellishment flatter your body and do not overwhelm your small frame. To that end, stay away from large flowers near the neckline or across the waist. Consider a strapless mermaid or trumpet gown.

Small busted

Flowers or other ornamentation around a strapless bodice will balance a pear shaped figure, bows or lace applique on a neckline can add shape to slim the torso. Consider a sweetheart neckline or a deep V-neck gown, which will accentuate the bust area.

Hourglass

These girls are fortunate to have several options. Try a V-neck or an off the shoulder number that will flatter a large chest, a dropped waist highlights a narrow waist, a Basque waist and full skirt slims the hips. You can also do strapless or cap sleeves depending on your preference.

Fuller waist

Try an empire gown, with the skirt flowing from just below the bust. This shape will create a long leaner silhouette. Also consider an A-lined dress or a dress that drops past waist and goes fuller thereafter.

Short waist

Try a princess shape to create a long, slim line. A high to low waist or empire front but lower is the back will also lengthen the torso.

Wedding Looks

Hair

Ever gone to a new stylist and walked out looking like a peacock or worse yet like someone just cut a bowl on your head? Now, for those of you who dream about those looks atop your head pardon my example. The only thing you need to remember is that feeling of disappointment you experienced when you had a service that did not thrill you.

You do not need me to tell you that how a woman feels on any given day makes a world of difference in how she carries herself. This feeling will increase one hundred-fold on your wedding day. Take the time to figure out how you envision yourself on your wedding day. You have to find a way to communicate that to your stylist. I found that the best way to do that is to have a few practice runs and a few photo ideas. It may be a pain but you will thank me later.

If you only take one thing away from this example let it be this, go to a stylist you *trust* for your wedding day look. If it is impossible to do that and you must invest in someone new, make sure you go to them several times prior to the wedding to make sure you both are on the same page. If you are doing a destination wedding and simply have no time to do it in advance, then start early and give extra time for any adjustments. Otherwise, my recommendation is at least three times. And for heaven's sake do not try anything dramatically new just days before your wedding. At the very least try it a few weeks before so that any mishaps can be tamed before the wedding.

Makeup
Since I have stressed the importance of the hair lets move on to make up. You should try out looks a few times before the wedding just as you do your hair. If you can have both done at the same time that is awesome. And take pictures. You will not remember all of the things you loved after the make up is off. You also may be so excited that you neglect the things that may have to change or be adjusted. If you are really detailed-oriented, you would make copies of it and paste it on a copy of your dress board. It makes the whole wedding seem so close and so much more real.

Manicure & Pedicure
All I can say is just do it! The cost is nominal and you will have these pictures forever. If you are dead set against it, at the very least find a nice clear or nude coat and make it as perfect as possible. Those hands of yours will show up in many a photo for years to come—so it will matter.

Dressing on a Budget
Many brides seek to save money on their wedding dress and that is a reasonable expectation. There are plenty of ways to save money in the dress department so that you can spend money in other areas. If you are looking for creative ways not to break the bank for your dress, there are a few options I recommend:

- Bridal discount stores
- Ready-to-wear tea length gowns
- Bridal shop sales or "trunk" sales. One or two times a year bridal shops will have sales to clear out any old stock. These sales yield deep discounts. If you think the dress will be outdated, consider partnering with a seamstress to add details that could update the dress. In the end you could still end up saving quite a bit of cash.
- Wear a family gown
- Resale shops
- Order bridesmaid dresses from national catalog (e.g. J. Crew bridal collection and Nordstrom Bridal)
- Rent gown or bridesmaid dresses
- Buy inexpensive ballet slippers for all the dresses
- Look for tuxedo deals because they are always around and the groom tux is usually free with a certain number of groomsmen tuxes.

Dress Saving Ideas

The best tip I can give you is to shop early. Next, know your budget before you shop. Tell your consultant what your budget is and take a good friend or your wedding consultant with you so that you will stick to it. Rest assured that a dress can be found on any budget. Ideally the dress should not exceed 10% of the overall budget.

If you are not looking for anything fancy but you still want something elegant many brides shop for bridesmaid dresses or prom dresses in ivory and white. Sounds crazy but there are some super-cute styles that may be just perfect for what you are going for in a dress. It is your wedding so go ahead and push the boundaries a bit with accessories especially in favor of your personal style. Here are some ideas to get you from beautiful to beautifully amazing:

- Vintage stores
- Sample sales at high-end stores and boutiques in your area. Word of caution: the sample sizes are usually for sizes 14 and under.
- Off season designs
- Mix up the fabric

HAESE
Photography

- Bridal outlet stores
- Antique veil or shorter veil or fancy hairpins
- Get jewelry from mother, grandmother or aunts. Something old or borrowed anyone?

Timetable for Dress Fitting

Start shopping for your dress as soon as you book your venue. Ideally, start no later than six to nine months before the wedding. When choosing your dress make sure your purchase at least six months beforehand. At whatever bridal salon you choose you will have to purchase it to size (read: your current size ladies). This will give you enough time for your dress to be created and delivered to the store and another few months for fittings and alterations.

Remember to shop for wedding shoes. Not just for you but your bridal party as well. Bridal shops make it so easy these days because shoes are simply dyed to match the dress. Voilà!

First fitting is usually 3 to 4 months before the wedding to allow time for alterations. Final fittings are typically done 6 weeks before the wedding and last minute tweaks are done the final week or so before the wedding.

Picking up your dress should be simple. Have your dress in hand no later than one week prior to ceremony. Keep it in a safe place free from excessive heat and definitely away from any foul odors. Have pets? For the love of all things good do not put it in a place where they frequent because the last thing you want is a dress laden with fuzz balls or smelling like them at their most private moment. As a final matter, you will also need to make sure that the dress does not need to be steamed or pressed just before the big day. Save yourself from that kind of stress!

Paying For Your Dress

Find out about special payment or layaway plans. When I was shopping for my own dress, I went to several shops and all but one had a legit payment policy. By legit, I mean I was sized and then put down a portion of the cost until the dress arrived and I could begin fittings. Remember the shop I mentioned earlier? The dresses in that shop were *beautiful* and came with the added bonus of the owner actually being the designer and the maker of these custom dresses, but she wanted full payment prior to any creation. That little tidbit stopped me dead in my tracks and ultimately, I opted to go with a shop with a more lenient payment plan to protect myself against any type of fraud or dress disasters. Be sure that the payment policy is something that you are absolutely comfortable with. I just preferred for both parties to share the risks and it is hard to get your money back once you put it all in one basket.

When you do find the right dress shop, and the perfect dress in your price range you should request a detailed description of the dress in writing. Most shops will give you a receipt for your purchase or a bill of sale. My advice is to pay with a credit card for greater protection instead of cash, checks or a bankcard. Also, check to see if your wedding insurance covers any dress mishaps.

Preserving Your Dress

So with all this wedding talk you probably have not even thought about preserving your dress, right? Well, lucky you that you are reading this! You need to make arrangements to have the dress preserved as soon after the ceremony as possible. It is best to have the dress repaired immediately following the festivities. Make it easy on yourself and ask your mom or a trusted friend to drop the dress at your cleaner.

By the way, there are lots of fun alternatives people are taking advantage of with their dress that I want to share. Some people go the traditional route and save the dress as it is for a future bride in the family, but there are plenty of options. Here are some really fun ways I can think of to make your dress go even further:

- Have it altered into a short style as a first anniversary dress;
- Use parts of it to construct an elegant evening gown;
- Use it as part of your wedding album;
- Create a memento board for your makeup room;
- Have it repurposed as a christening dress for your future little one or for a close family member.

These are just a few ways. The sky is the limit! If you have other ideas in mind, definitely do it.

Some Final Thoughts

I have girlfriends who know exactly what they wanted in a wedding dress and have been imagining it since they were little girls. Other girlfriends have no clue what they want. I was both of those girls! Granted, I had all these ideas about what I thought I wanted and had read all the magazines about what would work best for my body but when it came down to it, I ended up deciding on the exact type of dress I thought was not my style. I loved that I could be surprised because the dress fit my body and exuded exactly what I wanted for my wedding day. Here is my advice: definitely explore and find out the stuff you like and want beforehand but definitely be open to something new. Many brides know exactly when they find the right dress because they get very emotional seeing themselves. Other brides know the dress by the reaction of their loved ones. Whichever the case, you can trust that you will know when the right dress comes along.

I recommend visiting reputable bridal shops with knowledgeable salespeople and plenty of stock to choose from in your area. If you need advice on some of the better shops, talk to friends and family or just do an online search. The value of going to a fabulous shop is they tend to have knowledgeable salespeople, skilled seamstresses on site who can tell you the most flattering styles and silhouettes. Keep in mind that if this fabulous dress shop is in a large city the prices could be higher.

It is best to schedule an appointment and avoid "dropping in". This is one of the most important days of your life that you are preparing for so by all means schedule an appointment so you get the undivided attention and time you deserve. Overall, appointments are just easier and ensure you maximize your time finding a dress.

You should be comfortable taking advantage of your consultant's expertise. When you do schedule the appointment, be upfront about your budget. I recommend sharing your budget with the consultant early on if they do not ask. A skilled and resourceful consultant can find a dress on most budgets. If not, she will tell you that she cannot help and point you in the right direction. Equally important to sharing your budget is sticking to it. Be steadfast in what you can afford. It is only an injustice to you if you are wooed by the gorgeous dresses that cost $5000 more than what you can afford. My rule of thumb is I did not even *try on* dresses outside my budget. I know that I am spontaneous and spoiled and it would have been just my luck to fall in love with something I could not afford. Dress shops create an illusion but you want to remain firm.

Once you find the oh-so-perfect dress, get an alterations quote immediately and before buying the dress. Often times the alterations can cost a pretty penny so you will want to make sure that they are either included in the price or that the dress *and* the alteration fees still fit within your budget.

CHAPTER 5: *Venue Selection*

A venue is simply the place where your ceremony and reception will be held. Deciding on where to hold your special event is an important decision as it guides almost every decision thereafter. For example, if you choose a venue that is a private residence that can reasonably accommodate 150 guests, the venue capacity will dictate the maximum number of guests that you can invite to your wedding. In this section I will cover all the ins and outs of finding and securing the best venue for your event.

Finding a Venue

The venue and theme should work hand and hand to reflect you and your soon-to-be husband. If you are in the category of ladies who have thought about every detail of their wedding, you already know just the venue for your wedding. Maybe you have envisioned getting married in the church you grew up in or your favorite historic site, or even your parents' backyard. Maybe you have not thought about it at all, but you and your groom love a particular monument or met at a site where you would love to exchange vows. Whether you already know or you have no clue of what you want, my only advice is put a deposit on the venue the moment you figure it out. You would be surprised at how quickly that little church in the suburbs books up.

For those of you who have no idea where you want to get married, have no fear. The P3 book is here to get you thinking about it and before you know it you will hopefully have the perfect venue in mind. If that is the case start talking to people you know, especially those who were recently married or know someone recently married. These women probably looked at quite a few venues before they settled on something. They can be a wealth of information. If you have enlisted the help of a wedding planner you should be asking them these questions. My wedding planner was worth her weight in gold for all of the resources she brought to me. From florists, to caterers and everything in between, a wedding planner will have a few tricks and reputable vendors up their sleeve.

Now, lets figure out a few ideal venues! In the Resources section there is a worksheet to help you focus on what would work best for you. The questions will get you thinking about the places and activities that you and your soon-to-be love. Take some time by yourself or together and answer the questions with as much detail as you can muster. Hopefully, once you answer the questions you will begin to get an idea about the perfect place. Hint: as you think about places whatever gets your heartbeat going is usually a dead ringer of what you will love.

Continue to think about the questions and before long you will be on your way to finding that perfect venue for your big day.

What To Do When You Find A Venue

When you find the venue that you love start researching what it is all about. It was important to me to get an idea of what my guests would experience so I wanted to take a test drive of the venue as often as I could. If you decide you love it, make sure the basics are covered and then book it!

At the risk of sounding picky, I highly recommend that you make sure you check out the bathrooms in the space. While searching for a venue in a large city, I noticed that while some venues could accommodate up to 250 guests, there were often times only a small bathroom quite a ways from the main dining room. That was a red flag to me and I thought it could be an issue, creating long lines for my guests. If you are having a small reception then it won't matter, but do take that into consideration. And don't be shy about asking the guide or someone at the venue about it. Be direct and let them know what your concerns are. Since the venue holds events there regularly they can give you an accurate picture on how other brides have handled the issue or if it was an issue at all. My rule of thumb was always if there are 50 or more guests you need at least two restrooms or a single area that accommodates multiple guests.

Basic Venue Requirements

- – Size: should fit all your guests comfortably
- – Details: are linens included? Find out everything the venue will provide such as microphones, speakers, security, ramp for disabled guests and parking
- – Reserving your venue: most accept early reservations (12-18 months); ask friends and family about where they had their event
- – Who's in charge: you want a pleasant experience so watch and pay attention to the interaction you have with catering or on-site manager

- Can adjustments be made for inclement weather? Is the backup plan agreeable for you?
- Are there enough restrooms to accommodate your wedding guests?

One Venue or Two?

Next, you will have to decide if you will have different sites for the wedding ceremony and reception. Or if your venue is anything like mine, you can save time and money and hold both events at the same place. There are advantages to having the wedding and reception at the same place but it is perfectly fine to have the ceremony in one location and have guest travel to the reception site.

If you hold the ceremony and reception at different venues, my only advice is keeping the distance between the two venues short and sweet for your guests. That means no more than 20 to 30 minutes between the venues. If distance cannot be avoided make sure you give your guests a map and if you can afford to do so, a shuttle from ceremony to reception could ensure your guests make it safely and on time for your reception. Many of them will be traveling from out of town and may not be familiar with the area so a map or a shuttle would be more than welcome. The better coordinated this effort is, the more likely your guests will arrive at the reception quickly and ready to celebrate.

I was thrilled to find a venue to hold both my ceremony and reception. We chose a private estate that folks could drive to and with plenty of parking. If you are having a city wedding where parking could be more limited ask how parking is typically handled. We also booked multiple hotels but had our primary hotel 10 minutes from the venue, so we were able to negotiate the hotel shuttling guests to and from the reception site to the main hotel. That plan would make it easy and limit liability in the event guest enjoyed the reception beverages a little too much.

Selecting a venue that could hold both the ceremony and the reception could also cut cost. One venue means one payment as opposed to two. If you choose to have a ceremony in a church or public monument it can still be really affordable so do whatever makes you happy.

Qualifying Venue's In House Caterer

As discussed, some venues come with an in-house catering department and the bride and groom simple select which items will be served. In this situation, once you narrow down the reception venue be sure to go to dinner or attend an event there so you can get a feel for the staff and the ambiance. Also try going at the time your reception is scheduled. I also advise you to take pictures! I tend to go overboard with pictures but I do this for planning purposes. However, if you are not into taking pictures but have a great memory then you are amazing and should be proud. Nonetheless, you, your planner, or someone you trust should be with you. If your planner is with you they will surely take notes and a few pictures unless they are very familiar with the space. You can also check the venue website as they usually have a floor plan for you to use, which should help with any detail you forget.

Ask a lot of questions about the layout of reception. Make sure you can fit all your guests comfortably. Also make sure the reception site has a good traffic flow pattern. Make a list of questions for the site manager before you meet. Get details in writing about what the venue will provide and request a copy of the contract to take with you. Finally, understand your legal obligations if you choose the venue.

It goes without saying that if you hire a private caterer for your reception you need to check them out first. It does not matter how many people recommend them or the food, you need to try it for yourself to make sure you and your fiancé love it too. Many restaurants or the chef will offer a tasting. A tasting provides you an opportunity to try the food of your choice for a nominal fee. Be sure to ask if the tasting fee can be wrapped in the final bill should you choose them. It may seem small but every dollar counts when you are vigilantly sticking to the budget.

Last but not least, jot down a few notes about your first impression of the venue. What wowed you and what didn't? Most likely, your guests will also notice these things too so be diligent.

hile a ceremony may seem pretty simple in concept there is a lot that goes into making sure that it looks seamless. I recommend doing a program so you can start envisioning how the ceremony will go. As you begin to organize this part of the day, consider the following program outline:

HAESE
Photography

Processional

Traditional entry most commonly set to music where ushers will enter first followed by bridesmaids and groomsmen, either in pairs or in a single file, followed by ring bearer and flower girls, and then finally the bride with her father.

Greeting or call to worship
Master of ceremony or officiate will welcome guests and set tone for the overall ceremony.

Charge to the couple
This is where the officiate will share that bride and groom have come together to marry of their own free will and ask if you two vow, "to be your lawfully wedded..."

Readings & Music
If these apply, a couple may want a particular poem or scripture read that encompasses their relationship.

Presentation/giving away of Bride
This is the all-famous part where the dad, grandfather or whomever the bride chooses, is ceremoniously "handed" over to her groom.

Vows
There are so many options and most people choose one of the two: (1) write your own vows and speak directly to your soon-to-be, or (2) use the traditional vows. Whatever you choose, remember that the words should express your intentions to love, trust, and to honor each other. With personal vows you can also express how you two met, how you knew your soon-to-be was the person for you, or funny stories to shed light into your relationship. This is fun for guests who have not been around to witness the courting phase of your relationship. Later in this chapter, I give you a roadmap of how to craft your vows and make them memorable.

Exchange of rings
Bride and groom place wedding bands on each other.

Pronouncement
This is the famous phrase "I now present/declare that...are now married!"

Recessional
The grand exit by bride and groom, followed by parents, bridesmaids and groomsmen, ushers and remaining wedding party.

Choosing An Officiate

I recommend you meet with a few unless you already have someone in mind, like a minister who knows you, your family or your groom really well. There is no need to limit your considerations to clergy. Many modern weddings include a close family member or friend to conduct the ceremony and it is perfectly acceptable. It has become quite easy to get ordained for the day to perform a wedding ceremony. However, I caution against doing anything too over the top. This is your wedding, a very important day, and you do not want someone who is purely a jokester who does not know you well overseeing your day.

For a religious ceremony contact you or your groom's house of worship and see who is available on your day and time. If you are planning from afar, ask friends or family who are local to your wedding venue for recommendations or a good wedding consultant in the area. Check the yellow pages for a wedding consultant, as that could be a great resource as well. An interfaith ceremony may also require some planning. In that case contact both houses of worship to see if a joint ceremony can be included or just ask how interfaith unions have been performed in the past. While some faiths are stricter than others, most religious venues have already addressed the issue for other brides.

For a civil ceremony, contact the local town hall and they can tell you who is qualified to perform the ceremony.

Working With The Officiate

Strive to create an amicable relationship and making your officiate a close acquaintance or friend. You must have officiates consent to marry since he or she are the legal aspect of your big day. Usually, the officiate must complete the legal paperwork to validate the marriage in the state, otherwise your nuptials will not be legit. The absolute best advice I can give you is get officiate on your side by extending a lot of common respect and courtesy. It will go a long way towards your big day!

Writing Your Own Vows

Many couples chose to write their own vows and I have seen people do a variety of things. Usually, written vows tend to be more personal because the couple has taken time to speak from the heart. It could be heart-felt or slap your knees funny. It really just depends on the personalities of the couple. The decision of whether to use the traditional "to have, hold and protect till death do us part," versus writing your own vows is a very personal one. I was perfectly happy to have a traditional ceremony and do a short little speech at the beginning of the reception. This is a part of the day that you can really do however you want, but do make sure that you let your minister or whoever is marrying you and your groom know what you want. The last thing you want is to ask them to do something they are not comfortable with. Or worse yet allow them to prepare something just to find out you wanted something different all along. Communication is key here.

Nonetheless, it is very modern for the bride and groom to write their vows. This is often a good approach when you have a themed wedding or when you have otherwise infused your unique style into much of the ceremony or reception.

So what do you say if you are writing your own vows? Now, this very question and finding the answer is what prompted the more traditional approach during the planning of my own wedding. We could not figure out what exactly to say! It is sometimes a lot of pressure to try and write everything you love and adore about a person, and capture that sentiment in a 3 to 5 minute speech. I knew with all the nerves I would have going that day I wanted to just relax and let the minister do his thing. Anyway, if you are braver than me and mine (no shame in that!) here are some guidelines to help you write your vows and to wow your guests:

- Talk about how you and your fiancé met
- Talk about how the relationship transformed your life
- Talk about your love: symbols or common interests
- Tell any quirky or otherwise interesting story symbolizing the love you share or how you knew he/she was the one

Whatever you say, try not to ramble, stay on point, and make sure there are tissues nearby! You know *somebody* is going to cry, even if it ends up being you. People tend to get pretty emotional on the actual day and you want to be sure to get your speech out. If you are saying your own vows I highly recommend you having a microphone or printing the vows in the program. One of the things guest complain about most is not being able to hear such an important part of the wedding.

Receiving Lines

In even the most casual of weddings, a receiving line cannot be avoided. The receiving line is the time where the bride & groom (and sometimes joined by their parents or honor attendants) greet all of the guests who are in attendance. This is important so please make a plan for when your guests will have this time with you.

The receiving line need not be anything extravagant and it is commonly done immediately following the ceremony. If having the receiving line immediately following the ceremony is not convenient for your event just do what works best for you. Again, usually the married couple; their parents; and sometimes the honor attendants are there.

I have a huge family so I had some concerns with the receiving line taking a bit of time, so I planned a go to statement for any guest who attempted a prolonged conversation, *"hey aunt Such and Such, this is my best friend Aimee, thank you so much for coming, she will help you get to cocktail hour."* Taking the time to think about how to handle the situation gave me the peace of mind that I would honor my desire to greet each guest but also saves the married couple from spending 3 hours greeting everyone. Whew!

The Wedding Program

Once you determine what elements you want included in the ceremony, decide who will proceed over the ceremony and what you will say to each other, you will be ready to draft your program. A wedding program is a nice addition to your wedding service so definitely consider including this small, impactful touch. A wedding program really enables guests to participate in the ceremony by listing members of the bridal party. It is also helpful to include:

- Relationship of wedding party to bride or groom
- Interesting information about the family
- A note of thanks and appreciation to family
- Your new address
- Parts of service that some guests may not understand (for example, if you are having a Jewish ceremony and invite non-Jewish guests you may want to print a copy of the song translated so guests can follow along. This helps your guests understand the song's significance to you.)
- Wedding trivia
- Showing respect for a departed loved one
- Names of other wedding participants

The program is also a great way to introduce the key people in the ceremony to your guests. While you may know everyone in attendance, your wedding guests will not so this is an easy way to let everyone know who the major players are at the wedding.

Seating

Traditionally, the bride's family and friends will be seated to the left and the groom's family and friends on the right. Certain rows should be reserved for family closest to the bride and groom. If parents are divorced seat them in separate rows. If neither has remarried and they are friendly and amenable they can sit side by side. Rule of thumb is the parent who raised you is seated in the front row and the other parent a row or two behind. Everyone else is seated front to back as they enter the ceremony space.

At this point your ceremony should be good to go. Feel free to revisit this chapter again just before the wedding as a gentle reminder. In the beginning phases, things like the program and seating just will not be as important as finding an officiate to marry you and deciding what you want to say to each other, whether traditional vows or writing your own. Good luck!

CHAPTER 7: *Reception Site*

When I think of the best parts of the weddings I have attended it always comes down to the cake, the dress, and the food! So make sure you secure your caterer and venue early since the good ones tend to book quickly.

Preliminary Preparation: The Questions You Need to Answer

When I first got engaged I was so excited to see this new sparkler on my hand everyday that I barely thought about planning the wedding. Heck, I was enjoying the idea of *being* engaged too much! Even if you do not start planning every detail the day after you become engaged, do begin to think about what you want. Whether you have a solid idea of what you want or not, focus on events and food you like and that will be a great starting point.

One of the most important details of your wedding overall will likely be your theme, but if you've been diligent in reading this book, you have already began thinking about potential themes and how to execute it. But, if at this point you are still part of the clueless bunch the last few chapters will help point you in the right direction. Once you start thinking about the symbols of your relationship it is time to answer the questions that will bring everything home.

What is your reception budget?

At fifty percent of the total wedding budget, the reception is the most expensive item in the overall budget, so brace yourself for it. If at any time during the process costs start to mount you will either have to rethink the food and drink or cut down on the number of guests. The reception budget usually includes such line items as the food, beverages and site fee. Most venues have a site manager or someone similar assigned. At the very least an employee who is familiar with the venue will be on hand to assist and make sure the place is not damaged during your bash.

HAESE
Photography

How to incorporate the wedding theme at the reception?
The style of your shindig will guide the food and drink you choose. For example, if you and your fiancé are wine connoisseurs or love barns then that can easily be translated into a theme. My fiancé and I were in love with the urban cities where we grew up and both cities became our theme. You should feel comfortable taking whatever you love and making that a part of your wedding too. Unless you are from an ultra conservative family and must have a traditional wedding, the world is your oyster. Even if you must have a traditional wedding there are ways to incorporate a few items that still represent you.

What time of day will you get married? How long of a reception?
The amount of time you set aside for your reception will dictate how involved your food and drink options need to be. Generally, the longer the reception the more food and beverages guests will expect.

Many brides have a time of day they want to get married and of course the evening ceremony and reception is always popular. But do what works for you. I have attended several early afternoon weddings that were fabulous. The sunlight is certainly best during the day so keep that in mind for pre-reception photos. If you are a budget bride, an early afternoon wedding could save you some cash. Another bonus to an afternoon reception is that you can serve brunch food, a light lunch, or even just desserts. Folks will not expect a full meal that early in the day.

Most receptions last about 4 to 5 hours and that is plenty of time to get the reception activities done. If you are renting a space for the evening the contracts I found usually ran either in 6-hour stints or you pay for the entire day. The idea of the 6-hour time block is to allow for a one-hour setup and breakdown on the front and back end of the time block with 4 hours for the event. In my area, there were two Saturday blocks—10am to 5pm or 6pm to midnight—unless you rented the space for the entire day. However, if you have your event at a private residence you may have more flexibility as far as duration. Just be sure to ask your venue what time slots they have available or the amount of time the fee will get you.

Do you want any reception activities?
Reception activities are any entertainment that you provide for your guests during your wedding. For example, will it be a dinner party or will you have other entertainment in place? For my big day, I planned a photo booth with obnoxious props that represented both of our cities; a cookie bar for guests to enjoy between dinner and the cake cutting; a collage at the reception desk that guests could sign and write a message on while they picked up their table cards; and guests could also tour the venue during downtime. Also, I planned the receiving line just after the ceremony and followed by a cocktail hour, which can help you seamlessly transition from ceremony to reception. This will give guests something to do while bridal photos are taken. There is no obligation to have a ton of activities either. In the normal wedding line up there is already plenty to do, so feel free to do the tried and true if that is appealing to you.

Speaking of a reception activities, typically during the reception there will be a first dance, father-daughter dance, mother-son dance, toast, dinner, and cake cutting. These are some activities your guests can enjoy so feel free to count these as part of that activities list. Though it seems like a short list it takes some coordination to get it all done at a leisurely pace in just 4 to 6 hours.

There are many reception activity ideas from wedding shows on TV or bridal shows. I found the most popular to be the photo booths, dessert bars, miniature golf and other lawn games, poker and bowling. My suggestion is use the list you create in the theme worksheet (found in Chapter 15) and try to include some of them. It will provide guests a glimpse into your style as a couple and you are sure to have a great time at your wedding if the events you enjoy are included.

What size wedding do you have in mind?

The size of guest list will likely impact what you plan to serve, and how it can be served. If you are planning an elaborate affair with 250 guests or more then you might consider a plated dinner to avoid your guests waiting in lines forever. Or you may just increase the food options to ensure that people can move through lines quickly. On the other hand, if you have a more intimate wedding with 50 guests you may opt to have a buffet or a more elegant multi-course meal.

What does the reception site offer?

A reception site with limited kitchen facilities could impact your menu options. Many of the reception sites I visited had "warming kitchens" which meant my caterer would have to start preparing most of the food off site and finish at the reception site with ovens and simple pan-frying. Fortunately, this is quite common and most caterers are able to do this without breaking a sweat. Check the venue contract and be sure to communicate the kitchen restrictions to the caterer. You will also want to do a walk through prior to your big day. My caterer took pictures and had drawn the kitchen to scale even though she had done an event there years prior. She was smart to do this in preparation for my event.

If the reception hall does not come with an in-house caterer then you will also want to see what insurance the venue requires your caterer to carry. You should set an appointment with the caterer and the venue's management staff if the caterer has never worked there. During this meeting is also a good time for the caterer to provide proof that he/she can comply with food laws of the state as well as talk to the venue about your menu selections. A reputable caterer can perform these obligations without an issue.

Outdoor Event Considerations

First and foremost, try and prepare your guests for any event that is not indoors. If you are having an outdoor wedding or any part of the wedding is outside, you may need a rental agency or prop house for tenting and such. Your reception site should be able to make recommendation of companies who have worked the site before. If they are reasonable and available on your date, use them! Anyone who is familiar with the venue and the staff usually receives perks that are not afforded to newer or unfamiliar vendors. For example, one of the florists I interviewed had previously worked my venue and because she knew the site staff she was able to start setting up for weddings earlier than the contracted time simply based on her relationship. This will not always be the case but it is more likely if the vendor is familiar with the site and the staff that the vendor may have a bit more leeway.

There are several ways to let your guests know that your wedding or parts of it will be help outside. Consider including a quick line on the wedding invitation. I opted to put it on my wedding website and spread the word through the wedding party. No need to make a big deal about it, just let folks know something simple like "the cocktail hour will be held on the hotel patio where guest will enjoy..." You can also let people know by making a note of attire, "Guest will enjoy cocktails on the outdoor patio so feel free to dress to impress and comfy shoes will be provided." The main thing is to allow them the opportunity to prepare for the festivities.

Finally, you will want to notify your DJ of any special circumstances for the wedding. In particular, an outdoor event may require different equipment so you need to partner with your DJ and the venue to make sure you do not get stuck with an unexpected bill at the end, or worse having no music for your guests.

Seating

Whether you are having a casual or elaborate reception, you will need a seating chart for an organized dinner. Even if your reception is very casual, I noticed that guest tend to like when the bride and groom have taken the time to find a special place for them. Place cards can be so much fun for any theme. However, don't fret if you opt for just a plain white card with guest's name because most people are still honored when they see their name on paper. Trust me that little detail goes a long way so do not skip it unless your budget simply doesn't allow.

Where the bride and groom sit is totally up to you. The most popular options are a long head table or a sweetheart table. A **head table** is a table where the bride and groom are usually at the center surrounded by the wedding party. See the illustration below outlining who sits where traditionally, but again do whatever makes you comfortable.

Head Table

| GM | BM | GM | MOH | Bride | Groom | BMan | BM | GM | BM |

GM= Groomsman
BM= Bridesmaid
MOH= Maid of Honor
BMan= Best Man

A **sweetheart table** is just that—a table for two, where you and your husband are centralized in front of guests and are not joined by your wedding party. In this case, I have seen seating charts with the entire bridal party together or placed at tables with their dates and friends. It really just depends on your preference.

Bride   Groom

As a final note, be sure to treat your officiate as an honored guest. Make sure that he/she is seated in a prominent place. Though the parents of the bride and groom occupy their respective family tables, it is customary for officiate to be seated at the bride's parents table. However, if the officiate was recommended or is otherwise connected to the groom's family he/she should be seated at the parents of the groom's table.

Favors

Guests really look forward to this part of the wedding! As I was trying to decide what favors I would provide I gathered a *ton* of research from watching wedding shows, reading wedding and craft books, and talking to brides and vendors. Ultimately, I wanted something unique. Whatever you choose, just try to ensure your favors tie into your theme. The favor can also be a symbol of something significant to you and your fiancé. If you need suggestions, the following is a list of popular favors:

- Candy in elegant box tied with ribbon;
- Candy bar with Thank you note;
- Individual small candles at each place setting;
- Golf tees or balls with couples name for country club weddings;
- A single silk or fresh flower at each females seat;
- Bottle of bubbles to blow as bride and groom dance complete first dance;
- Wedding themed shaped cookies;
- Sunblock wrapped in bright paper, especially at a beach wedding;
- Key chains with couples names;
- Pears with "perfect pair" tagged on it;

- Holiday ornaments;
- Imprinted note pads.

Some brides choose to save money and eliminate favors during the reception. I definitely think having favors is a nice gesture and a great way to thank your guests for attending, but it is not necessary. Especially, if you are on a tight budget. I attended a casual wedding without favors and I did not even notice it until well after the wedding. Do whatever works for you and your budget.

Ways of Trimming Reception Budget

Consider hosting a reception outside of the normal dinner hour. Also, you may want to try a less conventional day than a Saturday. Think about morning, afternoon, or different days of the week, like a Friday or Sunday. Watch for sales on liquor and buy it in bulk. Use carafes of wine instead of bottles of wine. Open wine bottles can be wasted if guests do not finish them. Do a mini reception for a larger crowd with cake and punch and do a smaller, more elaborate reception for closest family and friends with dinner and dancing. If you need help serving dinner, check with a local culinary school. Many times if you offer a donation they will send a crew over to help. If you have a caterer they will likely have their own team.

Reception Planning

Benjamin Franklin once said, "if you fail to plan, you plan to fail." I believe this to be true and it was helpful for me to know deadlines for getting things done. Below is a quick list of reception items and the best time frame to get them done. You should also consult the "Ultimate Wedding Checklist" in Chapter 15.

Determine reception activities and quick sketch of events	As soon as you set date
Book caterer	8-12 months before wedding
Final menu selections	3-6 months or more
Beverage selection	4 months
Vendor check in	3-4 weeks before wedding
Reception seating	1-2 weeks before wedding
Final Guest count	1-2 weeks before wedding
Final vendor meeting for emergencies	3-4 days before wedding

Day of Reception Timeline

The bride, groom and wedding party should arrive before guests enter and begin to gather.

First hour

The receiving line is easy when it immediately following the ceremony. Or assemble a receiving line during the first hour and greet guests as they arrive. The band or DJ begins to play music. Drinks are poured and appetizers served to guests. Guests can also mingle and pick up guest and table cards. Photographer will be taking formal photos. If your photography package comes with a second photographer make sure one is capturing the cocktail reception and photos of the reception hall before the party.

After first hour

Guests are seated, wedding party is announced, and everyone takes their seats. Dinner begins. First course plated before hand. Wedding party is served first. Best man, maid of honor or parents offer toasts. First course is cleared and first dance happens, followed by father-daughter dance. Everyone sits for main course.

After 2.5 hours

Tables are cleared, cake cutting is done, dancing, cake is served and any other desserts are out for guests to feast on. This is typically when the official party starts.

CHAPTER 8: *Vittles & Libations*

This section covers three essential topics: (1) food; (2) beverages and libations; and (3) the cake. These truly are the main items to address and anything else is just extras (think dessert bar, cocktail hours, etc.).

1. FOOD

Choosing a Caterer

Find out what your reception site offers and then hire the type of caterer you need. Many venues have their own catering department so you just have to choose the meal from a pre-selected menu. Experienced full service reception planners can be great but just watch to ensure they perform each service well. You will want to see them in action *before* you book them and certainly before your wedding day. This is extremely important. Under no circumstances should you book a caterer without sampling the food they will serve your guests. The fee is usually nominal and should not be overlooked.

Scheduling a catering interview is a normal course of business. Make sure that you and the chef nail down the cost of any meal he/she is preparing for you. Many chefs will keep the cost general at first and that is ok, but you need to make clear what your budget is and the amount you plan to spend for food. As the wedding date gets closer, and within 90 days of the wedding, you should get an exact quote with a price guarantee based on the seasonal prices of food for your event.

Another important question is whether gratuities to the staff are included in the price. You will have to take that into consideration for the budget. Ask whether cost of bartender is included. This should be a line item within the catering contract if they are handling the bar, so just make sure it is there. The cost of a coatroom attendant, if needed, could also become important, as well as anyone else working during the reception.

I could not leave this section without addressing potential bumps in the road. Though you should reasonably expect everything to go off without a hitch, things happen so be prepared. Make sure the catering contract specifically outlines the refund policy, down payment, and payment schedule. Also check to see if there are any other miscellaneous payments that you could be responsible for before or after the event. This is what I call the "out-the-door cost" meaning what is the final price including all fees, services, and tax. Check the Resources chapter for further guidance on this.

HAESE
Photography

Selecting the Menu

If you have never planned a big event or ordered food for a large group you probably have no idea how to select the food for your wedding. Ask the caterer what is most popular or what he/she recommends based on your event details (i.e. theme, time of year, outdoor/indoor, time between events). Any reputable chef will tell you what will work best given the details of your wedding. Keep those things in mind as you plan your menu. Finally, unless you know exactly what food you want for your guests, ask the caterers you interview to come up with a sample menu based on your theme. From there you can start to adjust the menu to better suit your needs. If your parents, your planner, or a friend are good at such things have them help. At the very least you can run the menu by them to see if they point out anything you may have missed in the hustle and bustle.

Additional Menu Considerations

The type of fare you choose to serve is largely dependent on the time of day for your event. This will also determine how much food you will serve. For a morning wedding you can serve brunch, light lunch or in some cases just cake and punch. For dinner, guests will rightly expect something more substantial along with a dessert and possibly harder beverages.

It is perfectly fine to serve champagne and cake for an afternoon wedding. These are great ways to save money and still have an amazing event.

Oh, the budget rears its head again! Be wise and serve what you can reasonably afford. Practically speaking it just means you may serve chicken or fish instead of lobster and steak. If the food is tasty people will not care.

Ethnic and regional flavors are great if that is your background or if that is just the food you and your fiancé love! It also offers guests a twist on traditional fare and will make your reception memorable. If you are a southern gal—serve a southern meal! How tasty to have jalapeno cornbread, fried chicken and black-eyed peas? Yum! Or if the region you are getting married is known for something special find a way to include it. A friend of mine was getting married on the East Coast but loved her New Orleans roots. She was so clever in infusing New Orleans into her reception with pralines and mini king cakes as parting favors, and re-creating a popular street as the centerpiece of her reception. It was gorgeous and it was fun to feel like we were transported to New Orleans if only for a night.

Offering a Vegetarian Option

Most weddings include a vegetarian option for their guests. A quick note about vegetarian entrees: whether you are a vegetarian or not, *taste the entree*. When I first got engaged my fiancé suggested that we start watching wedding shows. Initially, I was not sure how helpful this would be but boy am I glad we did. I probably watched every single episode of at least 9 seasons! I learned a lot and took lots of notes about what I wanted my guests to experience. As a result, one of my priorities was making sure that the vegetarian dish was a legitimate dish that folks would enjoy. In my experience, it seemed that the vegetarian entrees served were more like an afterthought of side dishes instead of an actual entree. Your vegetarian guests should enjoy their meal just as much as the meat eaters. If you are not a fan of vegetables, and just cannot bring yourself to try a sample, bring along someone with a vegetarian-friendly palate. Then get their thoughts on the taste and their suggestions on improving, if necessary. Hopefully, you will have an amazing caterer who takes great care in all the dishes so everything, meat or vegetarian, will be equally delicious!

How will food be served?

Service is one of the most important factors when considering your caterer. Essentially, you will want to decide if you are having a sit down dinner, buffet, or food stations. Find out what choices the guests will have as far as entree and sides.

There are many ways to serve a meal and you can choose one or several styles for your big day.

- Buffet, usually a long table with a variety of food;
- Family style where large platters are brought to tables by wait staff, placed on the table, and guests then serve themselves;
- Food stations or individual buffet stations;
- Passed appetizers;
- Seated dinner/plated dinner;
- Service à l'anglaise where waiters serve from platters, approaching guests from the left. This is also called English service.

If you choose a buffet, consider having the same food dishes in at least two places at the reception site to help guests move efficiently. You want to avoid having your guests grab food and it takes too long to prepare their plates. There is nothing worse than getting back to your seat with a cold entrée.

What To Do With Extra Food?

If your wedding is like most, there is likely to be extra food by the end of the reception. You should talk with the caterer about how that extra food will be handled. You have paid for all of the food so you should certainly feel comfortable asking for any remaining food to be packaged and sent home with you, your parents, or guests. Or, if you are feeling generous many newly married couples donate extra food to a local shelter. That is an amazing gesture and again totally up to you. My fiancé was of the overindulgent kind so he wanted to make sure that a few meals went home with us. He wanted to avoid cooking later and to ensure we could take it to the airport as a snack before our honeymoon. I gasped at the idea initially, but soon agreed that it would be a lifesaver!

Last minute changes to catering

A final word on catering contracts—get *everything* in writing. I have included a brief outline in Chapter 15 but you should also be sure to read see Chapter 2 on Contract basics and the outlines throughout this chapter. Do not assume that the catering company or the chef will read your mind. If there is something that you want or need just be sure to include it in the contract. You should feel comfortable in asking for references from a few events they did recently as well. When you get these references don't sit on them, call them. Ask about the service and any improvements that could have been made. Also ask about how it was to work with the company or the chef. These are all important questions you should know the answer to sooner than later. If they have catered events recently it is also a good indicator that the business will still be there by the time your event rolls around. Now, of course the caterer/chef will give you the name and numbers of folks who will give them a winning review. That is to be expected. Just go in knowing that they are going to rave about the chef so you really just want to hear their experience as to the service and food quality piece and make sure no red flags are raised. If the red flag raises dig into it a little, while maintaining the positive attitude towards the caterer or chef. Try not to come across as if you are looking for something but instead come across, as though you want to be proactive in your own planning. Sites such as *thumbtack.com* and *yelp.com* are great resources for getting a list of reputable caterers or checking reviews of the caterers you may be interested in.

Finalizing the Caterer

When I started interviewing caterers I was able to eliminate some right away by looking at their menu options, or because they failed the taste test. But know that you will indeed find a few that measure up. When you do, here are a few questions you should ask to finalize your pick.

- Is caterer available on your wedding day?
- In this an in-House caterer or are you able to select your own?
- Can caterer perform within budget?
- Does the contract reflect all details of the service?
- What percentage of food over your guaranteed RSVP's will be provided? For example, lets say your caterer tells you they usually provide an excess of 10% over guest count. If your final guest count was 100 and 5 additional guests RSVP at the last minute then you are still ok because your caterer will bring enough food for 110. In that case there is no need to adjust your number. However, if more than 10 guests RSVP at the last minute, you need to up your final count and get it to the caterer quickly. Do not risk running out of food.

Interview Questions: The Caterer

If you want any exotic or non-traditional foods, you should definitely talk to your caterer. When talking to the caterer you may want to ask the following:

- Will caterer prepare family recipes to serve at reception, if applicable?

- Are linens included in catering quote?
- Are any decorative items included in the catering quote such as votive candles or colored napkins?
- Is gratuity accounted for in the catering quote? Is it a percentage or fees? Usually vendors are extended a 15% tip, which is paid during the reception by the best man. You will want to keep that in mind as you are budgeting.
- Will a tasting be provided for you and groom to sample? Is there a fee? If so, will fee be included in overall pricing when catering package is booked?
- How is the food presented? Inviting and makes you want to eat? Then this caterer should be a contender! (i.e. appetizers, fruit or cheese trays, meatballs, etc.). If nothing else it will give you an idea of the caterers presentation. Remember, if the pictures or food presentation does not make you want to eat or try it chances are it will not be appealing to your guests either.
- How much extra food will caterer prepare? Even though we discussed this before it's worth saying again, that you need to find out what the guaranteed number that the caterer prepares for. Get an actual guest count so that you are assured there is enough food.

2. BEVERAGES AND LIBATIONS

Whether you are having a full bar or limited bar you must include a non-alcoholic beverage option for your guests. You can do a specialty punch or just offer soft drinks, which are usually included anyway. Your caterer should also have this included somewhere in the service so make sure you check for it and that it is not a separate service fee.

HAESE
Photography

For the alcohol portion look into the state liquor handling laws; see who carries the responsibility for your guests during the wedding: the host or the company serving? You can also look to the venue contract. If it states that all alcohol must be purchased through catering then it means the risk stays with the caterer, which is why they must control the handling. The contract may also have some type of waiver indicating that bride, groom or hosts are responsible for their guests and outline penalty fees for violations while on site. Remember that wedding insurance may cover some accidents.

How many bartenders?

While planning my mid-sized event with about 125 people, my caterer recommended one bartender but I knew better. Fortunately, I had exposure to planning parties with a past job I held so I planned to pay the extra fee to have another bartender. I believe for every 50 guests there should be a bartender. My plan was that during down times the additional bartender would attend to the bridal table and when things got busy they would float back to the bar for back up. It seemed perfect and would ensure my guests never had to wait for a drink.

Different types of Bar Services

You will need to decide what type of bar service you will provide during the reception.

Commonly, a full bar includes gin; vodka; bourbon whiskey; scotch whiskey; tequila and rum. Your bartender or caterer will likely have these as well as the mixers on hand. If you are purchasing the alcohol, the above list will help you. The following paragraphs outline the specific type of services you can provide and any limitations within.

Limited bar

This is where you limit the quantity and type of alcohol served to guests. Offering beer and wine is an example and can be supplemented with soft drinks or punch.

Limited-time bar

Having the bar open or available only during certain times—like during the cocktail reception and after dinner. Host foots the bill.

Open bar

Mixed drinks, wine, beer, and soft drinks with liquors of your choice. Hosts or grooms parents foot the bill. This is the most common bar service at weddings.

Cash bar

In this situation, guests pay for their own drink. Thus, if guests want something besides soft drinks like beer and wine, they buy it from the bar. Keep in mind that your guests may have a very strong opinion about coming to a wedding and paying for a drink. If you can afford to offer drinks at your expense then I highly recommend it. If you just cannot afford it but want to make sure guests have the option, I suggest spreading the word prior to the event either through printing it on reception card or spreading the word via the wedding website, wedding party, or on the reception card. You should also consider offering a credit/debit option (yes, I know its called cash bar for a reason). It can cause issues if your guests need cash to drink but did not realize or forgot they needed cash beforehand. Do yourself and your guests a big favor and just communicate any limitations at the bar.

Bar Cost & Allocation

If you are paying for a catering company to provide the bar you may notice a few options. Having options is a good thing, however, you want to choose the option that will save you money in the long run. I will break down the options and then share how to approach choosing an option based on your wedding.

Per drink

Bar tender keeps tabs on how many drinks are served to each guest.

Open bottle/consumption: open and empty bottles of liquor are counted at the end of event and host charged based on consumption (number of empty bottles multiplied by fee per bottle).

Per person cost: a fee per person is outlined at your reception and is included in your contract. Host is charged a set price per guest. In this situation, it does not matter whether every guests drinks alcohol or not, you still pay a set price multiplied by the number of guests. Usually this balances out between those guests who are drinkers and those who are not.

For example, a quart of tequila is 32 ounces. If the bartender uses 1.5 ounces per drink that means any empty tequila bottle will count as about 21 servings. For per cost allocation, the bartender may use the same method. I preferred the open bottle or consumption since it was easiest and if you do not expect there to be much drinking then consumption option is also best.

Determining how much alcohol is needed for your event

As far as alcohol is concerned you just need to figure out whether you will purchase alcohol for the bar or will you pay your caterer to provide. For me, it really just came down to cost. I was incredibly fortunate because I was able to use my parents' military discount, and we could purchase bulk alcohol for much cheaper than any caterer could provide. You can find similar discounts at bulk stores near you or even purchasing online. Anyway, we opted to purchase the alcohol and turn it over to the catering company. Whatever you choose to do just make sure to check the catering and venue contracts to determine what your options are. Some venues that provide catering and some independent caterers will not allow you to provide your own alcohol.

If you decide to provide the alcohol you need to make sure you purchase enough for your guests. If this is done through the caterer, they will handle this. I was able to find several sites online that gave outlines to determine how much alcohol was needed (e.g. *apracticalwedding.com*), and there are even sites that allow you to plug in your guest count, duration of reception and it does the work for you. Luckily, I have done much of the work for you. Here is how to ensure there are plenty of libations to last during your event.

Serving Sizes
- 1 bottle of wine= 5 servings
- 1 case= 12 bottles
- 750ml of liquor= 18 servings (1.5 ounce servings)
- 1 bottle of beer= 1 serving
- 1 full sized keg= 165 beers

The all-important ratio
- Full bar: 20% liquor, 15% beer, 65% wine
- Beer and wine only: 20% beer, 80% wine

Consumption
- Calculate 1 drink per guest per every hour of reception. Keep in mind some people will drink more and some people will drink less but the above ratios should be plenty.
- If your guests list is more college kids or heavy drinkers you can calculate 1.5 drinks per guest per hour but you should make that determination based on your guests.

A Liquid Example
- Lets say your wedding includes 100 guests on a Fall or Summer Saturday evening with a start time of 5pm and ending at 10pm
  - 100 guests x 5 hours= 500 drinks
  - 500 x 0.20(%)= 100 beers or 9 cases of beer (always round up!)
  - 500 x 0.80(%)= 400 glasses of wine / 0.50 (servings per bottle)= 80 bottles of wine
  - NOTE: the trickiest thing for me was determining how much red versus white wine to purchase but I quickly learned that more people drink white wine. You can certainly do a 50/50 split if you want, otherwise plan on a 70/30 split.

- If you are still unsure ask your caterer to make recommendations or outline what you need. Be sure to give them a tip if they do this for you since you have essentially taken this potential money- maker from them. And if it gets too hectic pay the money and have your caterer do it! It is usually not exorbitant and quite common for them to handle the bar.

3. THE CAKE

Can I just say this is my favorite part of a wedding (you know besides the whole dress and love and happiness stuff?!). I am sure there are at least a few guests who feel the same way.

Finding a Baker
Even if you are not a cake person, you have to admit that since a cake has its own table and its own presentation it must be a pretty fancy dessert. What other occasion do you have a multi-

tiered cake with you and your groom at the top?! So invest in the best baker you can afford. There are tons of bakers out there. From small business home bakers to large scale professionals and you should try a few before settling down with one. When I was searching for my cake I knew I wanted something quirky and not so traditional, so I reached out to a well-known commercial baker in Baltimore that I had seen on TV. Turned out that the design was fabulous but my fiancé, parents and I were just not fans of the cake texture or taste. I was so disappointed because I just knew that this bakery would make my cake.

I recovered quickly—the very next day to be exact, and decided to go to some wedding shows since there are usually a ton of bakers with samples of their work on display. My fiancé was way more concerned with the samples than anything else but it worked out well because I met an amazing baker who was a great designer and made cakes that tasted out of this world! I was sold and booked her within 48 hours since she still had my date available.

Be sure to start early in booking the vendors who are most important to your day. The moral of my baker story is: do not be alarmed or shaken up if things do not work out exactly as you planned because it will happen. Just be diligent in finding the vendors who can make your vision come true and as closely match the dream in your head. If you trust yourself and the process, it will all work out in the end.

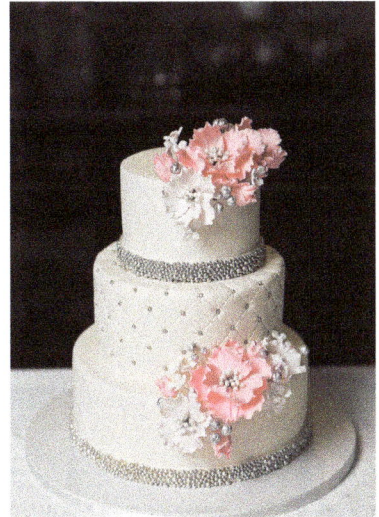

The Baker's Contract
Feel free to get creative with your cake. When you are deciding and interviewing your baker make sure your contract covers the following:

- *Fresh or Frozen.* Are cakes baked fresh or are they frozen? Frozen just means it is baked in advance and then frozen. I preferred a freshly baked cake but it is totally up to you.
- *Pricing.* Usually priced per person per slice and there is usually an average in the area. Prices can range anywhere between $3/slice to $15+/slice depending on the complexity of design, flavor and layers. This was a tough question for me because I wanted designer style on bargain prices. But I stayed within my budget and visited lots of bakers when I finally found someone who had the design capability without breaking the budget. So stay positive even if it takes a few tries. Budget NOTE: if your cake budget is $1500 and you expect 130 guests then your cake can't exceed $11.50 per person. That's actually a

pretty fancy cake so make sure that you get the final cost per person including cake and all fees (cutting, setting up, and delivery).

- *Delivery.* Will baker deliver the cake to reception or do you have to pick it up? I noticed that most bakers prefer to deliver the cake and assemble on site unless it is a relatively simple cake design. Pay the extra money for them to deliver so you do not have to worry about any cake drama on the big day. If a disaster happens, the baker will fix it at their expense and have all the knowledge and tools to get it done quickly. In my experience the fees were pretty reasonable, like $50-$100.
- *Deposit & Return.* See if cake stand has to be returned or any of the inner material. If so designate someone to return or make a plan to drop items in the mail. My experience is the baker gives you 2 weeks to return items so presumably if you are honeymooning for a week or so returning the base is something you can handle upon your return. The biggest thing is remembering not to throw it away. In my opinion, the caterer is in the best position to ensure it is safely tucked away so if you can swing it, throw in the few bucks to have her return it to baker. Chances are she will be best at ensuring it is sent damage free and on time.
- *Cake Cutting.* Will the baker stay and cut cake or assign someone? Many of the bakers I dealt with delivered the cake but did not stay to cut, so I just had my caterer do it. The caterer was experienced in cutting and serving, the fee was nominal and since she was running the kitchen her team could handle it flawlessly. However, if your baker includes a cake-cutting fee in her pricing and it is reasonably priced, take it!

Questions to Ask During Catering Interview

You want to know as much information about the service that caterer will provide during your wedding. Below are some questions I found helpful when I met with caterers. In addition, a Catering Contract Checklist is provided in Chapter 15: Resources as a quick reference. Below are some additional questions that could help you:

- Type of food service caterer is most comfortable with (buffet, seated, cocktail and appetizers);
- Type of plated service and whether first course, such as the salad, will be prepared in advance;
- Staff per guest needed (waiters, bartenders valet, coat check and restroom attendants);
- Liquor arrangements: who will supply, how many bottles there will be, whether you return unopened bottles for refund, hours of open bar, if wine and soft drinks how many bars there will be, policy for serving after dinner drinks and liquor;

- Whether musicians, photographer and wedding consultants will be fed. Caterer will probably require you to just include these folks in your final count as opposed to having to figure that out;
- Names of banquet manager and staff members who will be present during the wedding;

Negotiating and finalizing contract details tend to be the most stressful aspect of the wedding planning. Once this is done, you will be in a position to relax a little and just check in to make sure everything runs smoothly. Cheers to that!

CHAPTER 9: *Vendors*

Hiring the remaining vendors for your event are crucial decisions you will make. After all, you are entrusting the hired vendors to bring the vision of your dream wedding to life. In this chapter, I will guide you through the process of finding the right vendors, contracting with them, and working with them to ensure that your needs are met. This chapter is especially important if you are planning the wedding on your own. Though I do not want to cause any fright, this is such an important step in the wedding process.

I have separated this chapter into 4 sections: Florist, Musician, Photographer, and Transportation. These are the primary vendors that you will need to hire outside of the caterer, baker, and securing the venue. You will notice the information goes a bit deep into the details but have no fear. I have pared what you need to know down to information that mattered most to me during the planning process. Here we go!

1. FLORIST

When I was planning, one of the florists I interviewed gave me the best idea. She was extremely visual and realized what a clear vision I had in mind. As a result she requested to see pieces of fabrics I had seen and liked, pictures of the dress, the venue, the groomsmen suits, basically EVERYTHING. How smart, right?! What she did was put together a collage of my wedding vision so that she could begin to see what only my mind's eye had seen prior to that. Once there was a collage, I worked with her to move and adjust things to reflect what I had in mind. The result was a meeting of the minds! The vision was no longer just in my head; but it was a tangible picture of my wedding. This allowed me to clearly see what worked well and what did not. It was awesome! I cannot tell you how easy it became to decide last minute details and changes when you can just put a new idea up against a board and see how it fits. If your florist or wedding coordinator does not do this for you, take some time and do it yourself. It is a wonderful piece to bring with you to meetings when designing just about any element of your big day. It can also be framed as a memento later. I considered using mine as a reflection of my dream and then the actual wedding photos were the reality. It can be a really powerful tool.

Flowers may not make you go all warm and fuzzy but they mean the world to a wedding. Personally, it was just one of the budget items that I was willing to make sacrifices for because I knew it largely impacted the overall experience. Maybe you have a super talented friend or family member who can do this but if you are like the rest of the world find the best florist you can and book them early!

Again, flowers are what really make a venue pop. So whether you choose faux or real flowers for the day, be prepared for this line item, especially if you are using the real thing. From a budget perspective, be careful and diligent because this category of expenses can explode before you know it. I developed jaw-dropping syndrome when I first started pricing for my own wedding. But ultimately, when you find the ideal florist—the right look and the right price—it will be one of the best investments for your wedding. This little detail impacts guests the most visually (besides the food and dress).

Be prepared for *a lot* of flowers. Initially, I focused on the bouquets, ceremony, and the reception centerpieces but there is much more to this budget section. Below is a list of standard floral arrangements that you may need for your wedding. Check out the florist checklist found in Chapter 15: Resources. Now, of course if your venue is spectacular and/or outside with beautiful greenery or other decor you may be able to eliminate a few of these but here is the full list just in case.

- Bridal Bouquet
- Bridesmaid/Honor bouquets
- Jr. Bridesmaid bouquets
- Mother's corsages
- Groom's Boutonniere
- Groomsmen Boutonnieres
- Father's Boutonnieres
- Altar Arrangements
- Aisle decoration (sprays, pomanders, etc.)
- Table Centerpieces
- Head Table Centerpieces
- Cocktail Tables
- Reception Service Tables
- Cake Table
- Mantel Centerpieces, if applicable

If you focus on the above you should be in a good place to have your wedding covered. But keep in mind that every venue is different. The more decorated the venue, the less flowers you may need. The plainer the venue the more you will need décor and flowers to dress it up.

Finding a Florist

Now that you have a good idea of the importance of flowers in the wedding and what you will need, let's turn our attention to the person who will accomplish this task on your behalf. As a starting point, once you have found your venue and have evaluated what you may need, it is the perfect time to nail down a florist who can meet those needs.

If you have been a good bride and followed the advice of this planner, then you have set your budget early and before you make any florist appointments. My wedding planner had a wealth of resources about florists in my area. I had already met with one talented florist but wanted to see what else was out there before I contracted with anyone. The second appointment was with the most FUN guy who loved decorating and had an amazing eye for color and style. We had a fabulous time playing and putting things together. But as we moved along he had a very clear budget number in his head (the number I gave him) and he was able to tell me "close your eyes, that is way out of budget" and it kept me sane. I am telling you I am not even *into* flowers but when I start planning the look for my wedding it was, to say the least, addictive.

Ok, now how do you find someone as wonderful as whom I found? Ask people! If you have a planner he or she will point you in the right direction since they work with florists all the time. But you can also go online to wedding websites which usually have it broken down by city. Just be wary that the top rated florist is also top dollar. I also investigated popular review sites for recommendations, which were helpful, but ultimately I went with a recommendation from someone I trusted.

Once you narrow down the potential list of florists to a few, you must schedule a consultation. The upside to this is that you get a feel for their personality and work. The downside is you book your florist 6 months or more before your event and the flowers that will be in bloom for your wedding season are totally different from the season you meet with a florist. That fact was something I did not realize until our meeting. It was a frustrating process for me to only see colors and not have a firmer idea in the beginning but if you have some faith in your florist and remain confident that they understood what you want and envision, you will be fine. Remember it is pretty standard that while you talk concepts and color palettes up front, a meeting a few weeks before your wedding will allow you to actually see your wedding flowers and you can adjust closer to the date. The florist will probably have photos of his work from other weddings during your wedding season and that should help you get a visual of your flowers. So no need to worry if you are a control freak like me because it all works out in the end. If you could care less and just want the florist to do their magic, count yourself fortunate to have such a laid back attitude amongst chaos!

The good florists are taken early so when you find someone whose work you love and can perform within budget get that contract! The deposit is usually pretty nominal so you will not break the bank to get them secured. The florist checklist at the end will help in the process, but for now here are a few additional considerations.

What you need to know prior to meeting your florist

Be sure you let your florist know when to arrive at the venue and ensure the agreed time is before the photographer. You want the venue to look full and fresh in your pictures. Why take pictures at an empty and un-decorated place? But if this is just not feasible, many brides choose a park or some other decorated spot to take pictures before the wedding. Either way your photographer should have this in mind but just be sure that you are on the same page.

You will also want to think about the color you want included in your wedding prior to talking with a florist. If you just show up to a florist without a budget or without an idea of what you want you will be walking out spending thousands more dollars than you need to and will probably end up changing everything later down the road. That will get expensive. I also suggest bringing swatches of the bridal gown and the bridesmaid dresses so that the colors are more real for the florist. These are visual people after all. You can normally get dress swatches from the bridal salon for just a few bucks and it is worth the investment to have the exact color at the ready for your vendors to see, especially the florist. And if you have done your vision board that we talked about, you should certainly bring that along.

If the florist has never worked at the venue, make the trip. You should walk around with the florist so they have a better idea of what and where flowers work best based on decor already there. Usually, they are quite helpful in telling you what you can do to spruce up a place or tone down the crazy when and where you need to.

I've Narrowed Down a Florist: Now What?

When you find your flower god or goddess here's what you should ask/do:

- Are they familiar with venue? If not, ask them to visit with you so they know how it works and where the access areas are located. A great florist will always go to the venue to look at it well before the big day.
- Is there a formal contract? Do not be alarmed if the contract is not crazy in-depth. My florist gave me 2 pages outlining what he would do and it covered everything I needed, and I completely trusted him to create my vision.
- What are the delivery and set up fees? Is it a built into the quote?
- Will florist transport flowers from ceremony to reception site, if necessary? Make sure you get your money's worth.
- Let the florist know of any allergies you have.
- Take pictures from magazines or other weddings so florist has idea of what you like.

With multiple florist appointments under your belt, you may wonder how to determine when you have hit the florist jackpot. That just means what are the signs that you can readily see that are evidence that you have found a solid florist who can perform for your wedding. Below are a few of items that sealed the deal for me:

- He/she determines and shares with you the flowers that will work for your wedding

given the time of year and your wedding style.
- He/she offers suggestions and ideas.
- He/she can perform within your floral budget.
- He/she asks for pictures of your gown, bridesmaid swatches to ensure a seamless color theme.
- He/she explain the pricing system, including any deposit, payment schedule and final payment due dates.
- He/she provides recent references.
- He/she is willing to label corsages so you know who gets what
- Last but not least, it should be fun to work with them!

Budget Resolutions

In today's world of weddings, unless you are a celebrity or just have oodles of money to spend, there will be an area where you will need to budget or implement some cost saving measures. Here are some décor suggestions I learned while planning my wedding to trim that floral budget:

- *Centerpieces*: no need to use all flowers if you can supplement by stacking an item that fits into your theme. For example, if you are having a farm wedding then use honeycomb or jars of honey; or if you are having a city themed wedding use red apples in New York or peaches in Georgia. Also, candles are a beautiful and romantic item that lends elegance to any event. Another idea is to have staggered centerpieces. The short vases are cheaper than the tall vases so you can save money by having a few different sizes throughout. Some brides also use candy, colored rocks, or jewels!
- *Rented Centerpieces*: Check with florist to see what you can rent. Whether the rental be the vases or the actual centerpieces this can save money and you will be surprised about what value they can lend to your budget.
- *Ceremony*: consider large potted plants at altar and near entrance. It offers a pop of green and sets markers to let people know where to enter— serving double duty! Also, you can get ivy, garlands, or tulle and hang it from the pews or chairs adding just a little something to help it pop. Finally, you could also consider stringing lights or having solar lights or even lanterns to help the venue pop. Lanterns come in so many colors that it should be no problem to find a color to match your wedding and if not, a white lantern or candle just reeks of elegance and romance. You can find these at any online wedding accessory manufacturer or craft supply store.
- *Bulk flower purchases*: Check online search engines with simple keyword phrases like "wholesale florist" or "bulk florist" and check out the reviews—especially the negative

ones. See what the issues were. If the vendor consistently runs out of flowers or delivers late, skip them. A great website I found was *Aboutflowers.com,* which tells you how to work with your florist, contract tips and creative ideas. *Greatflowers.com* is also a great resource that allows purchases directly from growers and boasts a 50% savings.

- *Florist Schools/Students:* Check to see if there is a local floral design school. If you visit the school it is almost guaranteed that there is a shining star with an amazing talent and love of flowers. Many times they will produce your floral arrangements for cost of material and a great reference. Just know they'll want pictures since it is likely to become part of their portfolio. This is really an easy issue to address. Either have your photographer take photos that you can share with the floral student or invite the student to the grounds to take photos for their portfolio.
- *Non-Flower Décor:* Use balloons instead of flowers or greenery. They are cheaper, cover more space, add a festive party look, and can be assembled the morning of.
- *Local flowers:* Select flowers grown locally and in season and you'll save money.
- *Smaller floral arrangement:* Carry a single rose instead of a full bouquet and/or have your maids carry a single bloom down the aisle and maybe a flower in their hair.

Do not forget to talk to your wedding planner and florist about taking down whatever you put up. Sometimes the caterer will help with this but you have to make sure. Unless you are at a hotel or in a restaurant, you are still responsible for cleanup. Just make sure you have got that covered.

Where to Splurge or Save

I often wondered where are the best areas to splurge or save during the planning process. I learned that some areas are totally worth the splurge and other areas where a bride can be more economical.

Most brides want to splurge on the bridal bouquet because it shows up in so many pictures. I thought this was wise decision and it is true that it will be the most focal floral arrangement of the day.

I also recommend splurging on the ceremony flowers. This is an area where many pictures will be taken and you want great photographs. Plus, you can also take these arrangements to the reception site to save money. These flowers can be used on a large table, mantel, or in the foyer of the reception location. I would stay away from trying to use them at a cocktail reception if the cocktail hour is directly following the ceremony. It sometimes looks a bit thrown together if while guests are leaving the ceremony flowers are being taken down and rushed over to the next event.

HAESE
Photography

I opted to save on the bridesmaid bouquets. I kept it reasonable on these and added accents like pearls that would make them more impactful. If you think you need a way to make your bridesmaid bouquets pop, ask your florist for suggestions. My florist encouraged me to save money in this area but it is up to you.

I would certainly save when it comes to groomsmen floral arrangement and that is exactly what I did. Initially, I considered having the groomsmen have a consolidated version of the bridesmaid bouquets. This added up and in the end I opted to save money here. Instead of flowers I settled on a matching handkerchief and a handsome tie that matched the bridesmaids dresses.

You should also save on any floral arrangements for the flower girls. They likely do not even care about the flowers and you can do something simple like a flower in their hair or one of the flower headbands to create a cute, memorable look for them. You could even choose faux flowers for them to throw to save money.

Wedding Flower Priorities

Seasonal blooms are often the most elegant, simple and fitting solution and very economical!

You can mix and match flowers to create style or using just one variety of flower throughout can yield a romantic look.

Do not forget your wedding colors, of course! Shades of bridesmaid dresses and your wedding dress will likely work well.

Large spaces usually require large flowers or arrangements, whereas smaller spaces can do smaller arrangements or a few large arrangements.

Interviewing Your Florist

- Ask about a consultation fee
- Ask to see pictures of previous events. If you can see events from the same season as your wedding, that is even better.
- Most popular styles of bouquet? What's used most?
- What flowers are available?
- What flowers come highly recommended?
- Have they ever worked with wedding and/or reception site before?
- What will hold up best throughout the festivities?
- Will florist make suggestions based on my style, desired look and what is available seasonally?

- What's the policy for substituting if unavailable? Pre-approval?
- How to ensure flowers look their best? Misted and wrapped, etc.?
- When will flowers be delivered?
- Name of floral consultant for the day?
- Other decorations available? Fichus for example?
- Will you decorate cake and cake table?
- Do you preserve bouquets? Many brides have their bouquets preserved by freezing or drying as a memento. Ask your florist if they do it or if they can recommend a place that does.
- What additional costs beyond flower, vases, labor and delivery will I be billed?
- Rough estimate of total cost? Payment policy?

More General Floral Tips

Make sure bouquet is easy to carry. This just means the base should be comfortable to hold without any inconveniences such as thorns or loose ribbons that get caught on the dress or jewelry.

The ceremony flowers delivered should be well misted and wrapped in cellophane wax paper. This is pretty common and may be stated in the contract. If it is not I would ask the florist how they planned to ensure the flowers remain fresh looking as long as possible.

Assign a reliable friend or the on-site wedding planner to double check flower arrival and their condition. Someone should be on hand to make sure that everything goes smoothly with set up and that the venue looks perfect.

If you carry lilies in your bouquet, make sure the florist has removed the stems before jetting down the aisle because if left in it can stain the dress.

Be sure to wrap the hollow stems of flowers such as daffodils and euphorbia to ensure their sticky sap does not drip down your gown.

If getting married in summer stick with flowers that can endure the heat. High temps can cause fragile blooms like hydrangeas to wilt and sag. You will want to opt for heartier blooms like roses, orchids, and herbs instead.

A nice tip and a way to make flowers go even further is pulling together some of the flowers after the reception and sending to both set of parents the day after. You can also have florist send two new arrangements. You will be held in such high regard for this simple, yet thoughtful gesture.

2. MUSICIAN

This is definitely the part of any wedding that just reeks of fun. From the prelude to the processional (wedding walk) to the recessional (wedding exit), ceremony music, and of course the reception, there is lots of music to choose!

Weddings are so much more about the couple nowadays. Gone are the days when the bride must enter the chapel to "Here Comes the Bride." If there is a song that is special to you, then use it. But just a word of caution, be sensible. Keep in mind that your parents, aunts, grandparents and even your friends may still want a bit of nostalgia. My advice is keeping it sweet, simple and romantic is best. As long as you use that as a guide you should not ruffle many feathers doing something different.

DJ versus Band

Historically, more traditional weddings employed the use of a band. Nowadays, you will see more and more DJs emceeing the reception. The variety that a DJ can provide is obvious but if there is a great band in your area that you want to use, go for it because it is all about you and your groom.

If you enjoy live music then a band may be perfect for you. If you do not already have a band in mind, visit local clubs, check online and ask folks. Sit down as soon as possible to determine what they can do and you will want to see their range. Remember this is a group that will need to keep your dance floor filled for several hours so you want to make sure they have the material and stamina to make that happen.

There are some advantages to hiring a DJ for your wedding reception as well. DJ's tend to be less expensive but also less formal. Look for balance and variety with the DJ. He/she should be able to provide a good mix of fast and slow songs, have a good personality and excellent equipment. Ask for samples of their work— this could be a mix tape or a brief snippet online with past works. Just make sure it is a recent sample so you get a feel for what music is in their collection and the flow of music they will play.

While planning my wedding I decided to do a combination by having a band during the ceremony and cocktail hour with a DJ for the reception. Choosing the band was easy. My fiancé introduced me to a group he liked and when I heard them I fell in love with their sound too. Finding the DJ was not as easy and required a bit more investigation. Several DJ's were recommended and so we started going through the list. One DJ we heard about was known for a more local flavor which we thought would be great. But when we asked for samples, he had a much more aged sound than we wanted. Because people love him and he was on the club circuit, we would have relied solely on his reputation and would not have known that it was not a good fit. He was quite talented but better suited for a cabaret and less for our wedding.

Musicians

It is important to interview whoever will provide music for your wedding. Below are my five non-negotiable questions, but you should ask as many questions as you need to feel comfortable with the service. Here is my list:

1. How many weddings have you done?
2. What is the average size wedding that you have performed for?
3. When you notice that people stop dancing during reception, how do you adjust?
4. Can a wireless microphone be provided for speeches and toasts?
5. Is a gratuity included in the price quote?

You want to know if this is the first wedding that the musician has performed. Maybe the answer to that question will not impact your decision to hire him but you should at least know for your own sanity. While everyone definitely has to start somewhere and at some time it should be you who decides whether his or her first major gig will be your wedding day.

If the musician only does small events like lounges or weddings with 50 or less guests, that may be a significant consideration. Not only because he may be uncomfortable performing if your wedding has say 200 guests, but also because you want to make sure the equipment will be able to project throughout your venue. How silly it is to have a musician that only the people nearby can hear!

The reception and the cocktail hour are totally different experiences for your guests. Most often the cocktail music will be a bit slower paced and be lower in volume so that guests can actually mingle, talk, and hear themselves. However, the reception is more of a dancing atmosphere. The reception dance music is intended to get people moving on the dance floor as soon as the meal is done. Keep that in mind. Most musicians will ask you a bit about you and your groom's personality to gauge what will be best during both times. You can also choose your own music. I have recently noticed that brides ask guests to submit song requests. This is most often done via the wedding website and is yet another way to ensure your guests have a great time.

Having a microphone is so important but often forgotten. Have you ever attended a wedding ceremony and because it was a widely attended event it was hard to hear what the bride and groom were saying to each other? Whether you have or not, you can probably understand a guests' frustration if this happens. Weddings are fun and emotional and people want to hear it. Now, it may be less important if traditional vows are being done because people know those and can figure out where they are in the ceremony when you hear a word or two. But when the couple decides to write their own vows and you cannot hear it, it is like you missed a really important part of the ceremony. Trust me I found that out watching all those wedding shows because it happened time and time again. Guests would strain to hear and each time felt like they missed an important part of the ceremony when those special words could not be heard. The wireless microphone may only be used by the officiate in some cases, but nonetheless ask the question.

By now you have probably tired of me saying get everything in writing and ask what is included, but when everything is said and done you will be grateful that I tried drilling this in your head. Speaking of contracts, it is standard practice to leave a little something for each vendor, a gratuity or tip for a job well done. This gratuity is usually 10-15% of the contract fee and it not always clear within the contract. Don't assume that gratuity is included. If it is then you know that the musician is taken care of and it will be one less person the best man has to track down after the ceremony to hand an envelope. Either way, asking these questions will put you well above the learning curve and start you on your way to having a fabulous wedding.

Musical Selections

While all the vendors for your wedding are crucial, the DJ is the vendor who will likely have the most interaction with guests. The DJ introduces you at the reception, interacts directly with guests and gets and keeps people dancing, right? Well, my friend, take time and really get the right DJ and I cannot stress enough that when you find the right person book them immediately! You will find a checklist of what to look for in Chapter 15: Resources. However, before you book make sure you ask:

- What are you rates? Deposit required? Typically, a wedding band or DJ will charge for a block of time (e.g. 4-6 hours). You may find a few that charge by the hour but that can add up. However, I encourage you to negotiate an hourly rate should your event go beyond the scheduled time.
- Ask for a copy of the musicians or groups work and familiarize yourself with their sound.
- Check the contract to see how many breaks DJ will need and how often. Most importantly, see how music will play during the breaks.
- Will DJ announce you and/or help with bouquet toss?
- How long will they play/ DJ?
- If a style of music isn't working (i.e. people are not dancing or floor thins and clears out)

make sure they are comfortable with switching the vibe smoothly.

- Make a list of your favorite or "must play" songs. You may want to just give the DJ some guidance of the type of music you will want and let them do their thing from there.
- How much time does DJ require to get set up? Note: if you are having a cocktail hour in a different location, like outside, and the reception is indoors you will need to discuss how the DJ will smoothly transition.

Musician's Contract

Thankfully, these are usually short and sweet contacts. Just make sure that you review the Contract Checklist to ensure everything you need is included. As mentioned above, if your ceremony and reception are in a different locations and you are using the same musician at both you need to outline the above questions for both venues. You will find the checklist in Chapter 15: Resources to help.

You can keep all contracts in this book. When I was planning, I was so terrified that I would either lose a contract or that a freak accident would occur. That fear caused me to keep the originals in a file cabinet and keep additional copies in my book for easy access. My wedding planner also had a copy. Call it crazy but we never lost a contract!

The contract should also include what time the DJ can enter the facility to set up. The venue contracts should have all this in it. For my own planning, we had the venue for 6 hours, which is a tight schedule when you have the ceremony and reception in a single location. Thus, I made sure to hire vendors who had worked the venue in the past, and who could bend the rules a bit based on their relationship. Not that you have to do that but it could help you.

As I mentioned before, be sure to ask about noise control and speaker wattage. If you are having your wedding at a place where others may also be holding events you will want to comply with the venue's rules on noise control. The venue may require musician set up in a certain place and that the volume not exceed certain wattage. The suggested wattage is usually plenty for the capacity but just double check to make sure everything is in sync. You probably will not know how much wattage you need but your musician certainly should.

Finally, you want to make sure that the equipment that your musician uses is compatible with the venue set up. For example, if for some reason they do not have enough outlets or a functioning AV hook up you will need to address that. Make sure you clear that up at the on-set. If the DJ or band is not familiar with the venue you need to make sure you all take a trip over to ensure there will be no issues. Tedious but necessary on a day where you just want to come in, relax, and enjoy your big day.

3. PHOTOGRAPHER

Start searching for a good photographer early. Some brides have success doing an Internet search for reputable photographer/videographers but I found that the best recommendations came from friends and family. That is not to say you that cannot find some great folks on your own though. While researching photographers online I found this absolutely amazing, but pricey, cinematic photographer. A cinematic photographer just means that they create a short video of your wedding with music. It was beautiful and I definitely would have included it had my budget permitted.

Anyway, once I had referrals for photographers within my budget, I went to the reviews to see how other brides rated them. A photographer worth their name will also provide you with references and you should definitely call them!

When you do call references, my advice is that this is a two-part goal. First, when you call you are trying to find out how that person navigated around the guests at the wedding. A couple of pet peeves of mine were a photographer with a loud flash or click when they photographed. Another pet peeve was whether guests were still able to see during the ceremony and reception. You would not believe the things that can happen if you do not ask these questions. So make sure you ask how the photographer fit into the whole day. They should move around the crowd without intruding and guest should be able to enjoy the event with minimal adjustments.

Second, ask for the reference to send you a few photos. These can be emailed or they may even have an album online that can be shared quickly. When you view the photos pay attention to the feeling you get while looking at them. Do they make you feel that you were there? Can you see similar shots at your own wedding? Is the quality similar to what you want and expect? If any of these things are off you should pass and move on to the next photographer. You can also ask about whether the issues you have can be resolved. Be sensible though, it could be that the photographer had an off day or the shots you saw were from the assistant. Either way the quality should be consistent.

Interview Questions for the Photographer

Interviews are so important to me. I like to get a feel for the person I will work with and who will be around my guests. Most times there are no issues and it all works out just fine but as my luck has it, if I do not interview that will be the time a creeper shows up as a vendor. That is a no-go! So, here are a few questions that I made sure to ask the photographer:

- How many cameras does he/she carry?
- What type of lenses does photographer use? They should be high quality lenses and you will be able to tell the difference by the clarity of their photos.
- How many memory cards do they bring? The last thing you want is for the photographer to run out of space for all your amazing pictures. Most photographers carry at least 2 so just ask for him/her to bring an extra if he/she only mentions having 1 per event. As a frame of reference, 2-3 memory cards can hold about 500 shots.
- Are they a Full-time photographer? These photos will be with you forever, so make sure you are entrusting someone who is committed and passionate about photography. However, if you do opt for a part time photographer (because they are awesome) make sure you see their work and that the quality you want is there.
- Do they have a price list and outline of packages? Do not agree to a photographer without a price list up front.
- Ask what type of photography is their specialty? Photojournalism has become increasingly popular because these shots are candid. One benefit to this type of

photography is that you and your guests can enjoy the evening while the photographer captures all the fun. Traditional photography style is more posed photos, like the ones you'll take before or after the ceremony with your bridal party. The real difference is that in traditional photography people stop moving for the photo whereas the photojournalist captures people in motion (dancing, laughing, eating, etc.).

Scheduling Pictures

This can be tricky, but your photographer will tell you when is the best time to photograph based on the lighting. Take heed and you will have amazing photos!

Before the ceremony
- May get better pictures/helps relieve pre ceremony stress
- The photographer will likely still take candid shots in dressing room or at your home while adjusting your veil. Many brides have a picture taken with their mom helping put on the veil or otherwise helping the bride get ready.

After the ceremony
- Build some time in after the ceremony to take photos since it takes a lot of time to do multiple poses. This is where a well-timed cocktail hour will be beneficial.
- Everyone needs to be cooperative! Let folks know that photos will be taken immediately following the ceremony and receiving line. You also will want to give a meeting location so that no one gets lost or swept away.
- Taking good photos will definitely take time but should not take hours. Partner with the photographer, but typically you should expect at least 45 minutes to an hour for photos.

Before & After
- Best compromise if you do not want to see your partner before the wedding
- Work with photographer to help capture the essence of the day

Once you choose a photographer, schedule some time to visit the venue with them. After you have both explored the venue, you will need time to sit and discuss wants, needs and expectations.

Formal photos can be taken before or after the ceremony. It is totally up to you as to which you prefer. There is also a "first-look" which means the bride and groom get a private moment to see each other before the wedding. Usually during this time, a few pictures are taken as well. If you are the traditional bride you may skip this. I am one of those brides. I wanted my groom to see me for the first time as I entered, so we made the decision to take some group photos before the ceremony. For example, the bride and the bridesmaids at one time followed by the groom and the groomsmen. But you should absolutely do what you want to do. The next section outlines some photo shots that you may want to include.

Popular Bridal Party Shots

Bride Photos
- Couple with Bride's Parents, Grandparents, Siblings, Spouses and Children
- Couple with Bride's Parents
- Couple with Bride's Grandparents
- Bride with her Siblings
- Bride with her Parents
- Bride with her Mother
- Bride with her Father
- Bride with her Grandparents

Groom Photos
- Couple with Groom's Parents, Grandparents, Siblings, Spouses and Children
- Couple with Groom's Parents
- Couple with Groom's Grandparents
- Groom with Siblings
- Groom with Parents
- Groom with Mother
- Groom with Father
- Groom with Grandparents

Wedding Party Photos
- Entire wedding party and couple
- Bridesmaids with Bride
- Groom with Groomsmen
- Bride with Maid of Honor
- Groom with Best Man
- Bride with Groomsmen
- Groom with Bridesmaids

Additional Photo Poses
- Bride with flower girls
- Groom with ring bearer

- Bride with each bridesmaid
- Groom with each groomsmen
- Groom with ushers
- Couple with Officiate

Final Photo Considerations

Choose photography or videography whichever best suits your personal style. Many people have both and if you want both and have the budget by all means go for it!

Consider the keepsake factor of your photos. Think beyond the trends and consider what will be most meaningful to you and your families many years from now.

Don't neglect the lighting of the location. Indoor receptions are more difficult to shoot than an outdoor event. Consider having a few photos outside if possible.

Since this vendor will have a lot of contact with you and your guests so you should think about whether you can you work easily with them. Do they have friendly personality? References are definitely recommended here.

Photos and videos will be among your most cherished memories; so go ahead and invest in having photos that you will love but stay within the budget. Keep in mind the type of photos that you will get the best use of and avoid all of the other bells and whistles. For example, most photographers offer a CD or DVD, engagement shoot, online gallery, and magazine style album. Consider what you will use most and stick to those items during the ordering process.

4. TRANSPORTATION

If you are unfamiliar with transportation services or vendors, that's ok. There are many resources. I learned a lot, just by attending bridal shows. Transportation services include limousines, fancy sedans, and party buses. Transportation vendors are almost always represented during bridal shows and may even have a vehicle or two for you to look within. Whether you want a party bus, a limo or just a nice sedan you will have plenty of options. The most important thing is to make sure that the transportation carrier has the type of cars you want, plenty of them, and that they maintain their vehicles. Look online at the reviews and ask for references. You may even want to plan a visit to their lot to look at the cars yourself, which I highly recommend.

Services
It is never too early to book your wedding transportation. If you are getting married between April

and October booking early is especially important because bridal season is at its peak. When planning my own wedding at the beginning of October, I found that calling in the summer barely gave me enough time to get the vendor I wanted. I live in a large city so it may not be so bad if you are in a smaller suburb. Nonetheless, keep in mind that your spring or summer wedding may be competing with local proms and graduations. If you know the vendor you want, call them up and get that transportation scheduled.

Who Needs a Ride?

Typically, the bride, groom, bridal party, and the parents of bride/groom will need transportation. Providing a ride for the wedding party to the venue is sufficient. It is really the most crucial since you want to make sure everyone participating in the wedding arrives on time. No need to provide a ride for spouses or guests of the wedding party. Usually, they understand that they get to the venue on their own and the member of the wedding party will ride back with them. Voilà everyone is taken care of!

So, how do you find the right limousine company? Asking friends and family for references cannot be stressed enough. Nothing is better than having those you trust tell you about the service they received. They will tell you the good, the bad, and the ugly. For such an important day, that is what you need to know to avoid any mishaps. You could also do an online search and follow that up with one of the review sites. The combination of these two avenues will save you a lot of trouble and headaches in the end.

Another important aspect is finding a company that owns its vehicles. You will want to verify the service's license and insurance coverage; verify that they respond promptly and are on time. They should be professional with clean driving records (i.e. drivers do not have excessive speeding tickets or accidents). Another item to check off the list before making any deal is to inspect the fleet looking for modern cars free of scratches, dents, a pristine interior and take special note of the car smell. If it smells rancid or otherwise rank, well that just will not do. Keep in mind that some odors can transfer onto the passengers. Thus, the cars should be a clean and with a pleasant smell.

Pricing

This is another key part of this deal that I did not know until fully reading a transportation contract. The clock starts ticking when the car leaves the base and not when they arrive at the pickup location. If you find a service local to your venue you will save time and money. I would suggest finding a company within 5 to 10 miles from the hotel or ceremony if possible.

Look for package deals. If you find these folks at those bridal shows then you will likely get some type of discount. And you should! With all of the competition, paying full price is just silly and impractical. After that you just want to double check all the amenities included. Go with the company that is reputable and willing to throw in a few perks for your business.

While you are checking, see if they have runner service. Runner service means you can keep driver "on-call" to run home any guest. For example, you may want to account for those guests who have had too much to drink.

Be sure to check all of the above before going to contract. When you are ready to sign on the dotted line, be sure that you see the actual vehicle that you will be renting and make sure that is clearly stated in the contract.

Passenger Etiquette

Be respectful and kind to your driver at all times. This person will have a rare opportunity to see you at one of your most frantic and your most private moments with your bridesmaids and your groom. The secrets the driver keeps are definitely worth the niceties!

Also, find out whether or not the tip is included in the fee. You want to make sure you leave a good impression. It will go a long way since not everyone is generous. You might be surprised and get an extra trip to the hotel!

Finalizing the Contract

Here are the terms to look out for. A comprehensive transportation checklist is included in Chapter 15: Resources, but if you have these basic terms within the contract then you're in good shape:

- Type of car
- Additional options & services
- Expected length of service
- Date & time
- If you want a specific vehicle make sure it's in the contract. Also make sure to check the contingency policy

You should feel pretty comfortable with all the vendors at this point. If you have read through this chapter you will be armed with the information you need to find the right vendor and secure the ones likely to give you the best service for your dollars. Be sure to revisit this chapter as you continue to work with vendors to assist in overcoming any potential obstacles. And do not forget that there are several tools to help you in Chapter 15: Resources.

CHAPTER 10: *Invitations*

*C*hoosing invitations is a fun thing you will do early in the planning process. While it is definitely really exciting, it is also really important since the invitations set the tone for the wedding. Guests look forward to receiving the invitation as it solidifies the details of the event and is the guest's first glimpse into the wedding.

Who Gets to Invite Who

Ok, ladies this is a biggie. If you and your groom come from a small family then this part will be no sweat. If at least one of you has a larger than life family you are going to need a plan for the invite list. I only have two suggestions on how to handle this type of situation. Either divide the list in half and give one sheet to your groom and you keep the other or divide the list into four where you keep a list, you give a list to your groom, and give a list to both sets of parents with a specific number for each group to invite. As a caveat, be sure to determine how to count couples. If each person has room to invite 50 people, that could mean 25 couples or a combination of couples and singles. Either way, be clear about exactly how many people—total—need to be on that list.

The latter worked best for me. Since I am over the top organized, I created and printed out a numbered spreadsheet for each group of invites. I also had instructions that each married couple counted as 2 guests, otherwise when you get the list back it can be 30% to 50% more people than you planned. So be precise and clear about what you want back. I have included a sample template for you to use or you can use a computer program to make a quick spreadsheet.

Including Children as Guests

As far as invitations go the biggest dictators are going to be space, budget, mood, and your invite list. Who gets an invite is a very important decision and can include immediate relatives, close friends, the officiate, wedding party and speakers for the wedding. Your venue will largely dictate how many people can share your special day with you.

Whether to include children at the wedding is often an issue that arises. There are several ways to address this. First, if you are open to having children at the wedding or you are having a dry wedding then you can skip past this section altogether.

So, what if you only want to invite the children of immediate family? Or want an adult's only wedding and reception? Know that this can be a sensitive topic for some of your guests. However, anyone who has planned a wedding understands the costs associated with a wedding and your need for a strict headcount. Nonetheless, you may have to address why children are not invited. I recommend letting folks know from the beginning. The earlier you get the message out, the earlier you can address the concerns or pushback you will likely receive. Here is some guidance:

- Write on your invitation and reception card "Adults only"
- On the reception card include language that says " Mr./Ms. so-and-so and their adult guest _____ "
- Have your mother and bridesmaids share that since alcohol will be served, children have not been accounted for
- Explain to guest that it's your preference to have an adult event.

If you are uncomfortable telling folks that no children are allowed there is a compromise. Hire a babysitter or two and assign children to another room. Order a pizza or sandwiches with some soft drinks, water and sweet treats and let them have their own party. Parents can enjoy the evening knowing their children are in good hands and can pick kids up on their way out. In my mind that is a win-win situation. Fortunately, the venue I chose had a separate room that was perfect for such a thing.

If you do not have a room within the venue to use just rent an extra hotel room or ask the hotel for a conference room to use. The cost to rent a room, order food, and pay a few babysitters will likely come out much more cost effective than paying per plate for each child. Usually for every 10 to 15 children you need a babysitter—problem solved! If money is an issue; just have the parents pitch in a few bucks to help. It is likely they will not have an issue footing the cost to ensure their kids are safe and well cared for.

A little more about guest lists

Now there have been *many* arguments surrounding a wedding guest list. While planning my own wedding I often thought, "Are my parents crazy?! I do not even know these people! Why should they be invited?" Ok, let me say at the end of the day it is your day but I think there is a way to strike a balance in the overall list. Ultimately, you should feel that you have the support of those closest to you on your big day. Oh and did I mention this is usually the way the budget gets blown? If you stick to your guns with the list not only will you be patting yourself on the back when those vendor quotes come in (see Chapter 7: Reception) but you will also avoid you and your parents having a coronary incident (read: heart attack) prior to the wedding. Here is some guidance on keeping the overall list on track.

Wedding Size

Determine if you want a small, mid-size, or large wedding. Small weddings can range anywhere from 10 to 50 people. A mid-sized wedding is usually 51 to 150 people. Anything over 150 people is usually considered a large wedding.

Guest Count

Think about the ideal guest count you would like at your wedding. For example, do you want an intimate affair with just 50 of you and your groom's closest family and friends? Or do you want a mid-size wedding of 100 folks? Do you want a blow out bash that includes everyone in town that you both grew up with? Whatever you decide is fine, but *decide*. Remember to take into account your budget. If your budget is $10,000 and you want a wedding with 250 people, keep in mind that you may have to compromise on things like flowers or the quality and amount of food.

Plus One's

You may allow attached guests to bring their significant other. This is a nice gesture but certainly not necessary. However, members of your wedding party must be allowed to bring a guest. These people are spending hard earned bucks to be with you so the least you can do is let them bring their spouse or significant other. And of course, married guests are invited with their spouse unless the below exception applies.

Established Groups

If you are very friendly with your co-workers, you can invite them as a group. That cuts down on those extra plates you would otherwise be spending on their dates and also makes it easy to plan a table for them. For my wedding, we planned to seat all of my groom's co-workers together. That way it was like they had their own little office party at the wedding. We also had planned to allow their spouses to come as space became open.

So what happens when you have too many names on the list? Well, it's easiest to start eliminating categories of people like coworkers, distant relatives, acquaintances, and social associates. If you still want to invite them keep them on a back up list and begin moving folks up as you get invitation regrets (people who cannot come). Most invitations are sent out 6 to 8 weeks prior to the wedding but you can send them out a little earlier than that if you have a nice size waiting list. Furthermore, it is acceptable to send last minute invitations up to 3 weeks before the wedding.

Selecting the Perfect Invitations

Selecting your invitation can be really fun once you have determined the guest count and have nailed down a theme. Here are some tips to help you in selecting your perfect invitations.

First, *never* pay full retail price. There are plenty of discounts if you have signed up with invitation sites or for in-store mailing lists. Invitations set the tone for the wedding and reception to follow. The invitation also gives guests a first look at the type of wedding and the formality. Overall, it should indicate the mood of your wedding. Once you see a few styles that you like, request a sample so you can get a feel for the weight of the paper and view the available fonts. A discount code is usually included in the sample packet for future orders. I encourage you to order samples from a few different online outlets or visit your local stationary store. My experience was that once all the samples were in, it became easier to choose which product I liked best based on style, paper and font choices.

Next, make sure you get all the pieces you need. Invitations are not only a process to purchase but it also creates an experience for the recipient as well. Know that there are several pieces to the wedding invite that you send each guest. Even if you are having a casual wedding you will want to ensure your invitation packet is complete. Here are the parts to an invitation:

- Invitation
- Reception card
- Response card and return envelope
- Inner envelope (with all the above inside)
- Outer mailing envelope

Thirdly, you will probably get overwhelmed with all the accessories available. Accessories come in the tons, as you will quickly learn when you visit any retailer online or in-store. My advice is only get what you need, and know what you want. Conduct some research and search until you find the best price. My plan of action was if I fell in love with ANYTHING and it was unplanned, I waited 24 hours before purchasing. That way I had some space to decide. Trust me with wedding planning even the most aloof woman can get swept away! Ok, so here are some of the extras that you will find:

- Place cards: a card with guests name on it
- Table assignments: single card or enclosed in an envelope. Either stands or lies on a table outside of the banquet room and contains the name of the guest and his/her table number
- Programs
- Printed envelopes with return address or guest address. I definitely recommend investing in the pre-printed return address but I opted to have the guest's addresses done by calligrapher.
- Stamps
- Seals
- Postcards
- Save-the-Dates
- Informal note cards/Thank you cards
- Printed napkins
- Paper guest towels with your ceremony date
- Mini note pads

The list goes on and on. Literally, if you want any and everything printed with your names or wedding date, you could probably get it. Focus on the basics listed above and then you can add any extras based on what your budget permits.

Wording Your Invitations

The language of your invitation usually depends primarily on who is paying for the wedding. Hosts are traditionally the bride's parents, but nowadays the hosts can include the groom's parents or just the bride and groom. I have known brides and grooms who allowed their parents to host even if their contribution is a smaller proportion or nothing at all. It is totally up to you.

There are many different ways to word your invitation that lets guests know who is footing the bill. Here are the parts to include and a few examples:

Proper names of those hosting
Request line
List relationship of the bride to the host
Bride's first and middle name only
Groom's full name
Day of the week, day and month of wedding
Time of wedding and time of day
Name of the wedding location
City and state where wedding will take place
Reception line

Here are a few examples but you can also find tons of samples online.

Bride's parents hosting	Bride & Groom's parents hosting
Mr. and Mrs. William Santos	Mr. and Mrs. William Santos
Requests the honor of your presence	and
at the marriage of their daughter	Mr. and Mrs. Jeremiah Adams
Jane Elizabeth	Requests the honor of your presence
to Jonathan Patrick Adams	at the marriage of their children
Saturday the fourth of October	Jane Elizabeth
at six o'clock in the evening	to Jonathan Patrick Adams
Plaza Hotel	Saturday the fourth of October
New York, New York	at six o'clock in the evening
Reception to follow	Plaza Hotel
	New York, New York
	Reception to follow

Grandparents hosting	Bride & Groom Hosting:
Mr. and Mrs. William Santos	Ms. Jane Elizabeth Santos
Requests the honor of your presence	and
at the marriage of their grand-daughter	Mr. Jonathan Patrick Adams
Miss Jane Elizabeth	Requests the honor of your presence
to Mr. Jonathan Patrick Adams	At their marriage
Saturday the fourth of October	Saturday the fourth of October
at six o'clock in the evening	at six o'clock in the evening
Plaza Hotel	Plaza Hotel
New York, New York	New York, New York
Reception to follow	Reception to follow

These are just a few wording examples but feel free to use language that best represents you. Remember whatever you do just keep it classy. Invitation websites will offer more scripted language options so shop around until you find language that most represents you. A quick online search will help you find the language to address any situation if the above wording samples do not meet your needs. Whether your parents, his parents, an aunt, grandmother or you and your groom are hosting, there is a way to capture that in the invitation.

Ordering Invitations

This seemingly little detail was one of the trickiest I encountered. Just behind doing the actual guest list, be careful with your invitation proofing so that no mistakes are made to the language on your invitations. Re-ordering is not only a hassle because there is usually a waiting period between ordering and delivery, but it is also expensive to order a whole new set or even just a few extra invitations. If you end up having a few extras don't worry because you can use the extras in photo albums and other collectibles. Invitations typically get cheaper by each set of 25 so it is better to have a few extra than not enough. Ok, here is the official list to help ensure you get your invitation order just right:

- One for each invited couple, including the officiate and their spouse or guest;
- One for each attendant and their spouse or guest;
- One for each single guest over the age of 18, even if they live with their parents. For guests who are under 18 you can include their name on the inner envelope;
- Order 25 extra invitations and envelopes to have on hand in case of mailing difficulties, mistakes, and last minute invites. If you are hiring a calligrapher they will ask for extra envelopes so check with them to see how many extras are needed;
- Order an additional 25 envelopes as well. Mistakes will be made and even if you have a calligrapher address your envelopes, they will request extra envelopes from you. Just do it.

Timetable for Ordering Invitations

Ordering invitations and enclosures at least six months before wedding allows time for printing, delivery, proofing, addressing envelopes, mailing and the RSVP process. I ordered my Save-the-Dates much earlier and separately because we were planning over a year out and many of my friends traveled in the month my wedding was planned. I wanted to make sure they were able to plan accordingly. Things like wedding programs can be printed closer to the actual day once musical and reading selections have been made. Honestly, you can have really nice programs done at your local print shop. Most people will end up discarding these, leaving them on the seats or throwing them away altogether so no need to spend a fortune on them.

The calligrapher is important in the invitation process so give him or her at least 2 weeks for addressing envelopes. Talk with stationer to see if envelopes can be made available in advance so you can get a head start. That means you will hand them over 3 months or so before the wedding so the calligrapher has enough time to address them. That will allow enough time for you to get invitations out to guest's 6 to 8 weeks prior to the wedding.

Proofreading is really important at this stage. Carefully look over invite and outgoing materials and have someone you trust look over it too. The goal is to make sure you catch any errors. This is especially important with your master guest list. You want to be sure the calligrapher has no issues understanding names and addresses.

As mentioned prior, invitations should be mailed 6 to 8 weeks before the wedding. Announcements can be mailed immediately after the wedding or even the morning of.

RSVP's are usually returned 3 to 4 weeks before the wedding, which will allow time to plan your reception seating and to gracefully extend invitations to people on your back up or wait list.

Keeping Track of Invitations

One of the most important goals for me was keeping track of when invitations went out, especially if you have people on a wait list. If you need to follow up with folks about their attendance it can make it easier to decide who gets a call based on when they received the invitation.

Instead of creating multiple spreadsheets, include the stuff you will need on a single sheet. If you use a computer program such as Excel, you can use multiple tabs so that all the information stays together. Things will get more hectic the closer you get to your wedding date and the more hectic it gets, sometimes the less patience you'll have. Save yourself some time and stress and get organized early. There are forms for you to use in the "Resources" section.

Thank You Notes

When you are planning your wedding, one of the last things you think about is a thank you card. Nonetheless, these are so important. One thing to consider is where you would like gifts sent prior to the wedding. You want to make it easy for guests to get registry items to you, as most out-of-town guests will send gifts ahead of time to avoid traveling with them. Your local guests will bring their gifts in hand so you will still have gifts that show up to the wedding. Thus, it is smart to order a few thank you notes along with your wedding invitations. You can also purchase nice thank you notes from your local craft store. If you are super cautious you can place

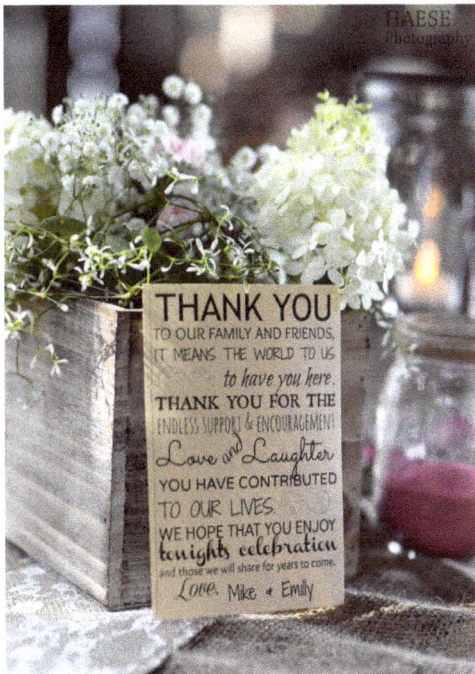

a larger order so that you send all the guests the same thank you notes. If you choose the larger order option, my advice is to get a fancy thank you note. You don't have to purchase a thank you card that is specific to the wedding. Just opt for a really nice design in white. If you keep the thank you card elegant yet simple, you can use these notes for years to come.

Guidelines for Thank You notes

Send out a note as soon as possible after you get a gift. My rule of thumb was ideally 3 days but no longer than a week after the gift is received.

Gifts received before the wedding should be signed with your maiden name. Do not get ahead of yourself and start signing with your married name. Mostly because you are not married yet!

In the note, thank the person for the specific, mention how you all will use the gift, and be sincere.

If you are unsure who sent the gift because the outer package is damaged or some well-intentioned sales associate was kind enough to black it out for you (yikes!) check the gift receipt or your register. If that doesn't work you can enlist your mother or a well-connected family member to investigate for you.

If you need to return a gift because you received two of the same item, wait a few weeks before returning or exchanging it. Typically, registry items can be returned within 60 days so that should be plenty of time for you to get any replacements. And you could change you mind and decide to keep it.

If you take heed to the advice in this chapter you will find your perfect invite, order the correct number of invitations and extras, and ensure that everyone is informed about the level of formality of the wedding. Hopefully, you will be rewarded with RSVP's that are returned in plenty of time. These quick responses show that your guests are excited to join you to celebrate your nuptials!

CHAPTER 11: *Registry*

ot sure what you should register for? Well, the answer to that will depend on your and your groom's stage of life. If you two are recently out of college then a traditional registry with all of the basic household items you will need to start a life together would work well. If you are well-established professionals then you may opt for some of the newer gift ideas like a honeymoon registry— where you and your groom pick your destination, hotel, and activities you will enjoy after the wedding and your guests put money towards those expenses. It has also been popular to let guests know in lieu of gifts they can contribute to a new home fund or donate to a cause that is important to the bride and groom. You could even do a combination of any of these.

Ideally, you want to make sure you have a good assortment of items that guests in any income bracket can afford. That just means if you are asking for that house and picket fence for your wedding be sure to throw in some towels and comforters too. Most stores will help you make sure you have a good assortment if you ask but if not aim to have a third of your registry under $50, a third for mid priced items (between $100- $250) and third containing the higher ticket items ($250+) so that all of your guests feel like they can contribute if they want to and not feel left out or obligated to go broke to attend. Aim for a gift to guest ratio of 3:1, so for every guest or couple have two or three gifts in your registry to choose from.

Speaking of those gift registries, historically it is less than polite to include gift registry information in the wedding invitation. People usually left that detail to moms, bridesmaids and groomsmen to spread the word. They were responsible for letting guests know where you and your groom were registered. I know it seems silly in this day of age but it can still be a touchy subject with those aunts and uncles in your family who are used to things a certain way. Nonetheless, things have changed and I have seen several wedding websites have a tab with registry information as well as convenient ways to shop online. The decision is yours how you choose to let guests know where you are registered and you should not have to worry your pretty little head over that too much. You already did the hard part of selecting all the items for your new life, now you just need to sit back and look pretty!

There are a host of places to register from department stores and cookware stores to big box stores such as Wal-Mart and Target. The possibilities are endless. As I mentioned above this could also include the newer registries ideas, which you could find with a quick Internet search.

Following are just a few items to get the ball rolling of things you may need for your registry. This is no way an exhaustive list. Your list should contain things that you and your groom need to start your new life. As a final note, look for online availability and numerous locations. Many of your guests will ship gifts directly to your home prior to the wedding so a store with online or ship to home availability is significant. Other guests will shop once they arrive. Basically, you will want to make it as easy as possible for your guests to shop for you. Ok, here's this list:

- Fine china
- Everyday dishes
- Silverware & flatware
- Glassware
- Sheets & pillow cases
- Comforter & duvet covers
- Towels
- Table cloths
- Placemats
- Napkins
- Porcelain enamel items (figurines, clocks, etc.)
- Copperware
- Kitchen appliances
- Cookware
- Wall décor
- Wine
- Carpet or rugs
- Outdoor patio furniture
- Sporting tickets
- Gift Certificates

Registry Etiquette

- Spreading the word: Even though putting registry information in the wedding invitation is taboo, it is usually fine to let folks know where you are registered via word of mouth and on a wedding website. If you take the traditional route, email the names of your stores or websites to your bridesmaids, the best man, family members, and anyone hosting a shower and let them spread the word for you.
- Gifts of money: if you would rather receive cash rely on your attendants to discreetly let

folks know.

- Duplicate gifts: If it is certain household items that you can use—like sheets or wineglasses, I would suggest keeping it. However, if you really do not want the item, exchange it quietly a few weeks after wedding.
- Damaged gifts: see if store shipped or mailed it by an individual. If it was sent from your registry call customer service and arrange for a replacement and do not mention the damage to the purchaser. If individual mailed it look for post office insurance stamp and call the post office. If its not insured, I would just try to exchange at whatever store it came from and again avoid mentioning the damage to the purchaser.
- Postponed or cancelled wedding: if your wedding is postponed you can keep any wedding gifts and send announcement to guests. If wedding is cancelled, each gift must be returned to the purchaser.

Recording Gifts

When you receive a gift, check the attached paperwork to ensure that you have received all the boxes and items sent. Save all enclosed cards or mailing labels in case you need to return or exchange. Devise a method of record keeping for gifts (see Chapter 15). Do not rely on computerized registries through the store. Keep your own system and use store registry as a backup resource if needed and if helpful.

For each gift record the following: name and address of sender; gift description; thoughts on the gift; store; date of arrival; date thank you note sent. A consolidated list is included in the back of the book.

Takeaways

- Register 4 to 6 months before wedding
- Avoid putting registry information into wedding invitations if you can help it. Instead put the registry information in shower invitations, other pre-wedding events or on the wedding website.
- Periodically check your registry the weeks leading up to wedding. Most people will shop 2 to 3 days before wedding. However, some folks will send a gift directly to the registry address. Update registry as needed.
- Find out how long registry will be stored in system in case you have people who want to purchase after wedding day. If it is a relatively short timeline you may want to mention that on any communications. For example: "Bride and groom have an open registry until [insert date] at the following stores…"
- Register for a variety of gifts in a wide price range with an emphasis on mid-range. Be

sure to list several less expensive items like kitchen gadgets, place mats, and wine for guests on a budget.

CHAPTER 12: *Special Issues*

*E*ven though this is a touchy topic, I would be remiss if I did not mention other areas of potential drama. The funny thing about weddings is that when you tell folks you are getting married, it brings out all sorts of crazy in otherwise stable-minded, supportive people. Do yourself a favor and take some alone time to plan out what you want everyone to do and have a clear vision. It will save you some stress in the long run.

One of the most difficult things I had to do was decide tasks for the bridesmaids and groomsmen. Deciding on the food, venue, and even the attire was literally a piece of cake for me since I had a pretty solid idea in mind. Anyway, I have taken some time to write down just some of the duties for everyone in hopes that it can help you. This is by no means an exhaustive list but it should get you thinking about all sorts of stuff you can enlist people's help with.

Bridal Attendant Roles

Maid of Honor Duties
> Address envelopes, if no calligrapher
> Receive wedding gifts
> Shop with bride
> Plan bachelorette party
> Dress bride for ceremony/veil
> Hold bride bouquet during vows
> Sign wedding certificate

Best Man Duties
> Lead organizer of the bachelor party
> Signs wedding certificate, if applicable
> Ensure groom gets to ceremony on time
> Pay professionals/vendors during reception (driver, officiate, wedding coordinator)

Bridesmaids Duties
> Pay for their wedding attire
> Help run bridal shower

Record gifts at bridal shower
Help prepare for wedding ceremony
Tell guests where bride & groom are registered
Handle meltdowns of other attendants or guests
Damage control for any challenging family or friends

Groomsmen Duties
Rent formal wear
Escort guests to their seats
Transfer gifts to secure location

Parental Roles

This is one area of business I knew little about beforehand. Besides paying for stuff what else would they do, I asked myself (jokingly, of course)?! Turns out there are quite a few duties entrusted to the parents and it is a good idea to get them on-board with their roles so that you can make any adjustments should you need to. Here are the tried and true:

Mother of the Bride
- Official hostess of your wedding but her duties vary based on where wedding takes place and amount of free time she has
- Help compile guest list and arrange ceremony and reception details
- Shopping for wedding dress with bride and her maids
- Act as official host of wedding day events
- Invited to most pre-wedding parties
- Chooses her dress first, then informs the groom's mother of her selection
- Seated in the first pew on the bride's side of the aisle
- First guest to be ushered out after recession is over

Father of the Bride
- Official host of the wedding
- Helps with wedding plans, including preparing maps and directions for guests
- Gets fitted for formalwear that matches wedding party
- Riding to the ceremony with the bride and escort her into ceremony site
- Walk bride down the aisle
- Make toast or welcoming speech
- Last to leave reception site
- Dances with daughter during reception

Parents of the Groom
- Cohost the wedding, if applicable
- Contacts bride's parents to let them know they are pleased about upcoming marriage
- Provide names, addresses and phone numbers for guest list
- Consult bride's parents on proper wedding attire
- Attend pre-wedding parties
- Host the rehearsal dinner the night before the wedding
- Seated just after mother of the bride
- Greets guests

Divorced/Unmarried Parents
- Divide the duties between the parents and you can even do so for the biological and stepparent.
- Parent who raised you sit a few pews back
- Try not to put divorced parents together in the receiving line. Even if on friendly terms because guests may get confused or misunderstand the situation.

Child Participants

Wondering how you can get the children in your family involved but maintain the elegance and fun in your wedding? Well, here are a few jobs that the little guys and gals can do with big returns:

- Ring bearer
- Program attendant
- Coat checker (ages 10+)
- Assistant gift attendant
- Candle lighter
- Altar boy or girl

Alternative Roles

If you have more family and friends than you know what to do with, like nieces or nephews for example, and want them included: have no fear! I have a few quick fixes for those last few folks you need to grant a wedding task.

When planning my own wedding, I did not realize how important it was to some of my family members to have a role in my wedding. It was a really sweet problem to have but an issue nonetheless. So when I found myself in this situation I started researching all the potential roles that could possibly be a part of a wedding. Sure enough there are plenty of tasks:

- <u>Ceremony ushers</u>: people who pass out programs, mass books, or yarmulkes before the ceremony. You can also have them pass out birdseed or bubbles to toss at bride and groom after the ceremony. If you have just a few people to place have them pass out both. If you have a good number divide them up and have some pass out programs and others put the post-ceremony items on the seats or as guests enter the ceremony.
- <u>Singers/Poets</u>: if you have someone close to you who is especially talented singer or poet include that in the ceremony or reception. My only advice is do not put someone at the microphone just to be nice, they need to be talented. You do not want your guests to suffer, right?
- <u>Scripture readers</u>: whether you are having a traditional church ceremony or not, you can always use someone to say a good word! Whoever it is, have them read the verse to you or in front of a small audience to ensure it is the right fit for the ceremony (can be heard, articulate, etc.).
- <u>Guestbook attendant</u>: Greets guests as they enter ceremony or reception site and asks guests to sign the book. Put it in safe, designated place once ceremony is over. It also should be present at the reception site for those that arrived late or otherwise just did not get an opportunity to sign prior to ceremony. No need to make one person stand there for the reception. If you have a 4-hour reception designate 2 people for the first hour go around collecting any new names and them let them enjoy the rest of reception. Have a cousin or trusted friend to oversee the guest book at the reception. This will help you remember all the people you met that night. There will be so much excitement going on it could be easy for things to get blurry, especially after the honeymoon.
- <u>Birdseed, petal or bubbles attendants</u>: Distribute seeds, petals or small bottles of bubbles to guests so that bride and groom can be showered as they exit. Check to see what your venue will allow. The venue I chose would not allow birdseed or petals so we opted for bubbles and it was an easy compromise that worked for all parties involved.
- <u>Gift attendant(s)</u>: directs guests on where to put any gifts brought to the site. You always hope nothing bad happens but to be on the safe side just be sure that someone keeps an eye on gift table, especially if your venue hosts several weddings or events at the same time. Deliver the gifts to a safe place once reception gets underway or after cocktail hour, if applicable.
- <u>Lady in waiting/personal assistant</u>: I chose my nieces to be my personal assistants so that they could spend the most important parts of my day right there with me. It was also nice pecking off orders without blinking too. This is a coveted position so be sure they

understand that.

- <u>Chaperone for your inappropriate "Uncle Ernie"</u>: we all have that relative who we just have to invite because its totally proper but the thought of leaving them without a leash just gives you hives. If you do not have one of these family members, I want you to get on your knees and thank the high heavens *right now*. As for the rest of the world, you can assign your nephew, a reliable friend, or cousin, or the wedding planner to keep an eye on said relative so that you can get back to business of enjoying your special day.

Sticky Situations

You may run into a less than ideal situation during the planning process. It is completely normal and a bit rare to have no drama prior to your wedding. So, just expect it in case it happens! Here are a few examples of typical issues that could arise as well as solutions:

- You have 2 sisters and you cannot decide who should be your honor attendant. If you do not want to choose have them both! If you choose both ladies to represent you during your big day just divide the honor duties between them and ask both of them to stand with you.
- You have a sister but also a best friend who is like a sister to you. You can ask both or just choose the one you are closest to. If your BFF is your honor attendant because that is who you want standing beside you, DO IT. More likely than not, your sister will be over the moon that she gets the coveted position as a bridesmaid. If she has trouble getting excited about it, by all means explain how important it is to you to have her there with you. If one of them is married you can also ask one to be a matron and the other a maid of honor.

Thanking Your Wedding Party

Did you know that it is commonplace to give gifts to the people who participate in your wedding? I am an overly hospitable person so I would have done so even if it were not commonplace. You should certainly try to give a little something to the attendants and wedding participants as well.

Basically, anyone in your wedding and especially those that contributed financially and who stand with you and your groom during the ceremony should be extended a gift. Specifically, that means your honor attendants (Maid/Matron of Honor and Best Man), bridesmaids, groomsmen, ushers, flower girls, and the bride and groom's parents. Some people have asked me if its necessary to give the groom's parents a gift if they did not contribute financially. If your budget allows then I would include a gift to his parents even if they just showed up to the wedding. Think of it as an investment in your future in-law sanity. These are the people you will be tied to for the duration of your marital life or their natural life, so why not make a small gesture and reap the benefits of being the, "thoughtful, lovely woman their son married?"

By the way there is no set gift for these folks. Instead you should just strive to get something that is meaningful to you or just something you think they would really enjoy. However, I did get each group the same gift to avoid any favoritism. For bridesmaids some typical gifts are jewelry, stationery, or a gift certificate. Since my girlfriends and I love wine (and even the harder stuff), I considered giving them mason jar shot glasses, a nice set of wine glasses or jewelry to wear with their dresses as well. Do whatever feels comfortable and just keep in mind: keep it tasteful and keep it within budget.

Potential Attendant Gifts

To help you figure out exactly what to get your folks, I am sharing a list of popular items. Below is a list of some pretty awesome gift ideas for men and women:

- For a traveler, an overnight bag or nice leather passport holder
- Wind chimes
- Books
- Gift certificates
- Jewelry
- Champagne and/or wine glasses
- Swiss army knives
- Cufflinks
- Monogrammed wallet
- Engraved money clip
- Travel kit
- Engraved calculator
- Jewelry box
- Baskets with soaps or perfumes
- Charm bracelet
- Music box
- Lingerie
- Book with personalize message
- Gift certificate for massage

If you have children in your wedding and want to give them a little something for their help there are several ideas for them as well:

- Mug with their name
- Games
- Stereo headset
- Videotape or movie
- T-shirt

Food for Thought

Your wedding party should be folks you are most comfortable with. Use good judgment and common sense when you choose to include children. There are several tasks you can allocate to friends and family so they feel included. Be careful about what you allow friends and family to do, just keep in mind some tasks need to be left to the pros.

Rehearsal Dinner

Finally, let's discuss something fun that you do not have to totally stress. The groom or his parents plan this event. Feel free to let them know what you want but give them some freedom too. Know that everyone will want to contribute a little something to the wedding and this is a great way for the groom's parents to do so. And if you are wondering who should be invited, here is a quick reference:

- Wedding party, including their spouse or guest
- Parents and siblings of bride
- Grandparents of the bride and groom
- Out of town family members
- The officiate and their spouse
- Musicians performing at wedding
- Parents of the flower girl and/or ring bearers
- Anyone else you would like to attend within reason

Use the rehearsal dinner as a way to introduce people and thank everyone for coming to your wedding. It is important to create a festive atmosphere. Keep in mind that this could be the first time when both families are meeting each other. Include the wedding party, but no need to invite young children if you do not want to. Again, an informal meal is fine just make sure folk's are comfortable. Many times once people meet at rehearsal dinner, they are friendlier at the ceremony and reception since they have some exposure to each other.

The best rehearsal dinners are informal, relaxed events. Consider a picnic, pizza party, cookout, or a restaurant. For my rehearsal dinner my fiancé planned to do it at our favorite local burger spot. Now this was no fast food joint. Instead, it was a really trendy spot in the Capitol Hill area. Even the President and many popular celebrities frequented this local gem. It was perfect because it was casual, fun, and the food was totally approachable for our guests. It also had chicken and vegetarian options. Go ahead and make suggestions, especially if the groom's parents are not from the area. Tell them your favorite local spots and why. Let them decide where they are most comfortable holding the dinner. The only thing that matters is that the food is great and people are comfortable.

On a final note, if you are wondering if you need to have a rehearsal dinner agenda the answer is: yes, but it is super easy and fun. No need to be intense. Below is a simple program for an easy rehearsal dinner:

- Introductions: bride and groom could do this jointly or separately
- Thank parents, family, and friends for their love, encouragement, and support
- Thank out of town guest for coming to wedding
- Give wedding party their gifts
- Take time for toasts (grooms father toasts bride, then the couple and anyone else)
- Eat, dance and enjoy the night before your big day.

CHAPTER 13: *Guest Information*

Wedding Website

About 9 months before my wedding I began a wedding website. At first the site started out as a way for me to keep guests informed because it was easier than answering a ton of phone calls and emails. A wedding website also gave me an opportunity to build excitement around my big day while engaging with guest early on. How amazing is that, right?

Ever been to a wedding where you are curious about who the bridesmaids and groomsmen were? If you are anything like me I enjoy being familiar with the characters at an event. Thus, one of the unexpected bonuses of creating a wedding website was how awesome it was to acknowledge and celebrate my wedding party. I absolutely loved writing their profiles and sharing stories of how we met or otherwise funny anecdotes. It was also a way of introducing the wedding party to the guests. And believe it or not guests love it! They feel like they are getting to know the wedding party and it makes them feel like an insider. Creating a wedding website for your guests is also an incredibly inclusive process. There are several sites out there. You will see at least a dozen sites pop up if you do an Internet search. Just be sure to read the reviews and pick the website that best suits your needs. Remember, guests love to have information about such a joyful occasion.

When People Arrive Have a One-Pager Ready

It was important for me to make guests feel included throughout the wedding process. Even if they do not take part in any of the activities it just feels festive to know there is someplace you can go to share all the fun with people who are in this city to have a wedding! No need to do anything fancy, you can literally print these out from your local printer. When you do, here are some things to include:

- Activities
- Time and address for each event
- Shuttle info, if applicable
- Personal note from couple
- Attire for each event

- Directions
- Area activities for guests outside the wedding

Welcome Kits

Who doesn't want a goodie bag?! Of course, everyone likes to receive a gift! Do not think you need to break the bank with this kit. You can truly fill it with whatever you want and it can just be a little something that really gets the festive mood started. Including a welcome kit is also very classy. Here is a list of what I planned for my welcome kit:

- A note from couple
- Itinerary for weekend
- Map showing ceremony & reception
- Emergency phone numbers
- Small gift items, like something to eat. Something like a granola bar or if there are local foods items you could also include that since it will be super economical and readily available in the area.
- Something regional like a figurine or keychain
- Bottled water
- Mini wine or sparkling grape juice

Keeping Guests Informed

I have always thought it was really important to make guests feel included and a wedding newsletter or agenda can do the trick. Send a newsletter closer to the wedding date. The newsletter can be sent by mail, emailed to guests, or posted on your wedding website. The newsletter should include details about parties and other events, weather conditions, hotel information and maps. Leave copies of any wedding agenda in each guest room, and with both sets of parents so guests have easy access to the information or someone who has the information.

Newsletters can also provide a list of babysitters or share information about where babysitting services are available for parents who have traveled with children. This is especially important if you have an adult's only wedding. For my wedding, I mentioned the venue had an extra room that was perfect for babysitting and came equipped with a large open space and a bathroom. It was a goldmine. And since a family member worked at a daycare I knew we would be able to find experienced childcare professionals at an amazing rate. Even if you do not have someone in mind reach out to the local day care facility near you or even some teenagers in your neighborhood who babysit and pay them to watch any kids at the wedding. Just make sure to coordinate with the childcare providers to determine what activities the kids will do while adults are entertained elsewhere and how to handle any emergencies that occur. It is also a nice touch to list the babysitter's qualifications.

You can also announce the activities you will have at the wedding or save it for a surprise altogether. The decision is totally up to you and there is no right or wrong answer. As for activities for adults during your reception, think about the overall experience. I wanted to definitely have some order but also wanted a relax vibe. We decided to have a few interactive activities (photo booth, cookie display, sundae bar), a fabulous DJ and an open bar so people who just wanted to dance and get their groove on could do that.

My fiancé was a great planner so he was in charge of finding activities for folks to do outside of the wedding. We planned to provide maps from the local airports, how to get to the venue via train or a cab and also listed stuff going on nearby. That way when guests arrived they knew how to get around and aided guests in getting familiar with the city.

Chapter 14: *Family Affairs*

There are so many wonderful things about the prospect of marriage. As the bride and groom you should fully enjoy all the festivity surrounding this joyous occasion. I truly encourage you to maintain and protect that joy throughout the planning process.

HAESE
Photography

Keeping that in mind, you should know that everyone in your life might be a bit emotional as well. Specifically, your union may bring up some unexpected feelings from some of the people closest to you. Do not be alarmed if this happens. It is absolutely normal and happens to most brides. Below are some common situations that you may experience. Tread lightly and be sure to remember that these are people whom you love and hopefully all will be well in the end!

Mothers/Mother Figures

It is common for moms to feel like they are losing their girl and the bond that has been established. Know that it is totally understandable that you want to make your own decisions regarding the wedding, but also be open to other people trying to help. Know that ultimately you will have the final decision, but keep an open mind for some potential great ideas. Be patient and kind with your mom and try not to be too hard on her. Remember, your mother absolutely loves you and wants you to be happy.

Fathers/Father Figures

Fathers play a very special role and keep in mind that he may be somewhat jealous of your groom no matter how much he likes him. This is because you are probably daddy's little girl. It may be difficult to adjust to the idea that he has to give up his protector role. It may also be a little sad so tread lightly. With dads, my suggestion is to ask if he wants to help (music, talk with bartender about drinks to be served, etc.). My dad loves to eat so I invited him to all of the tastings and even had him design a little system to determine what everyone liked best. In the end, having my parents sample the food and really enjoy it made it easier for them to pay for that catering bill! Finally, keep your dad or father figure informed of decisions you have made. Ask advice and counsel for anything that is of interest to him.

Your Future In-laws

Be sure to include them and get them involved as much as they want. It's also a good idea to keep them informed of what is happening and where. Because who has not heard stories about awful in-law situations? No one, right? Well, I was determined to be different and I wanted to set the tone early. So from the very beginning of the planning process, I tried to include my groom's parents in many of the fun elements of the wedding planning. For example, after my floral consultation I sent my future in-laws photos of all the things we put together and asked what they thought. I also had the mothers and fathers choose the corsage they wanted to wear. These little things allowed my in-laws to keep abreast of the planning going on and helped them to feel involved and included (I hoped!). Nonetheless, it is important to remember that even though you have so much going on as a bride, it is never to early to start establishing the relationship with the in-laws.

Siblings & Close Friends

You may also need to exercise some patience and kindness with your siblings and very close friends. While they are certainly happy for you there may be some underlying issues that cause hurt feelings or otherwise peculiar behavior once you announce that you are getting married. This could be true especially if you have a sister or friend who also want to get married. Focus on the opportunities to share this experience with your nearest and dearest and they will likely be happy if you are.

Keep in mind that even if things get a little crazy, you are planning your wedding and everything and everyone will be fine.

CHAPTER 15: *Your Ultimate Resource Guide*

We made it to the end! I hope you found that all the information within has been an enormous help to you. I would love to hear from you about how your wedding turned out and any feedback you have about your experience using this planner. You can post your comments on the website or send your comments via email.

In this chapter, you will find all the forms discussed throughout the P3 system. You should feel free to write on these or for the cautious bride, make copies. You could also create your own forms using a software program.

Good luck, thank you for using the P3 planner for your most special day and I cant wait to hear how it goes!!! xoxo

Ultimate Wedding Checklist

Below is a checklist to help you keep track of the growing list of task leading up to your wedding. There are blanks for any additional task you need to add.

12 or more MONTHS BEFORE WEDDING	
✓	TASK
	Announce engagement in local paper or social media
	Choose potential wedding dates
	Determine budget and contributors
	Choose your wedding party/ask for participation
	Purchase wedding magazines to narrow down your wedding style
	Get engagement ring insured
	Purchase wedding insurance
	Take engagement photos
	Start reviewing/designing Save the Dates
	Begin compiling guest list (divide into 2 or 4)
	Research ceremony and reception venues
	Research wedding planner and vendors: photographer/videographer, caterer, musician, baker, venue, florist
	Start searching for dress style ideas
	Order Save the Dates
	Begin thinking about bridal party attire and accessories
	Book ceremony and reception venues

10 to 12 MONTHS BEFORE WEDDING	
✓	TASK
	Book officiate
	Begin booking vendors: photographer/videographer, caterer, musician, baker, venue, florist
	Narrow down dress and veil options
	Establish fitness routine
	Establish skin care and beauty routine
	Research hotels near reception venue
	Finalize guest list
	Mail Save the Dates

8 to 10 MONTHS BEFORE WEDDING	
✓	TASK

Continue booking vendors: photographer/videographer, caterer, musician, baker, venue, florist

Shop for wedding gown and bridal party attire

Begin nailing down invitation design

Begin thinking about potential guest favors

Research wedding day hair and makeup styles

Meet with officiate to discuss pre-marital counseling and ceremony ideas

Reserve any rentals (chairs, linens, lighting, décor, etc.)

Begin planning honeymoon

Schedule reception menu tasting

7 MONTHS BEFORE WEDDING

✓	TASK

Begin looking at cake styles and schedule tastings

Schedule dress fittings

Choose groomsmen attire

Book any remaining vendors

Book transportation

Purchase wedding bands

Finalize wedding invitation and order a sample from vendor

Begin building wedding website

6 MONTHS BEFORE WEDDING

✓	TASK

Order wedding cake

Choose flowers for wedding party, venues, cake and attendants

Book honeymoon flights and hotels

Order wedding favors

Order thank you cards

Start pricing potential rehearsal venues

5 MONTHS BEFORE WEDDING

✓	TASK

Coordinate with hotel about setting up a reservation website for guests

Begin writing down items in a potential welcome baskets, if applicable

Prepare playlist for DJ

Order wedding invitations

Assist in deciding rehearsal venue

Make a list of potential registry store items

4 MONTHS BEFORE WEDDING

✓	TASK
	Finalize items for welcome baskets, if applicable
	Continue working on playlist for DJ. Update from wedding website
	Book hotel room for wedding night
	Finalize pre-marital counseling schedule
	Determine what type of first dance you will do
	Book dancing lessons with dad
	Register for gifts (at least 3 retailers)

3 MONTHS BEFORE WEDDING

✓	TASK
	Give master guest list to calligrapher, if applicable
	Map out reception seating
	Experiment with hair and veil options with a stylist
	Finalize ceremony and reception entertainment (readers, photo booth, etc.)
	Start practicing first dance
	Start practicing father-daughter dance
	Assist in booking rehearsal dinner venue
	Purchase toasting flutes, serving pieces, guestbook, flower basket, and ring-bearer pillow
	Finalize reception menu with caterer

2 MONTHS BEFORE WEDDING

✓	TASK
	Mail invitations
	Order wedding announcements, if applicable
	Draft/work with caterer on menu cards, if applicable
	Assist in ordering rehearsal dinner invitations
	Ensure you have system in place to start recording RSVPS
	Begin writing vows, if applicable
	Review ceremony details with officiate
	Outline wedding programs
	Apply for marriage license
	Finalize wedding day timeline
	Finalize playlist with DJ
	Finalize fittings and attire for wedding party and parents
	Send wedding day schedule to vendors and officiate

Share honeymoon itinerary with designated family or friends

Decide on your something old, borrowed and blue

Book spa and beauty treatments for yourself and bridal party

Book wedding day transportation, if you haven't already

Purchase gifts for attendants

Review wedding program

Make any reservations for wedding weekend activities (i.e. bridal brunch, etc.)

1 MONTH BEFORE WEDDING

✓	TASK

Map out reception table placement, including head or sweetheart tables

Designate where bride and groom's parent tables will be

Call vendors to confirm date, times and location. Communicate any changes

Final dress fitting

Double check honeymoon and flight reservations

Pick up wedding bands

Pick up marriage license

Pack for honeymoon

Write thank you notes for gift received

Follow up with guests who haven't RSVP'd

Address invitations for anyone on the wait list

Order wedding day emergency kit online

2 WEEKS BEFORE WEDDING

✓	TASK

Give final guest count to caterer

Check registry to ensure you don't need to add anything

Begin breaking in wedding shoes

Get final hair cut or color, if applicable

Send final playlist to DJ

Delegate wedding day duties: gift table and guest book attendant, etc.

Designate someone to return tuxes, rentals, and any tending to wedding dress

Send directions or addresses to wedding day transportation driver

Double check hotel blocks to get final guest room tally

Cross-reference hotel list with RSVP list

1 WEEK BEFORE WEDDING

✓	TASK

Prepare final payments to vendors and cash tips for service personnel

Lay out wedding clothes

Give any last minute directions to wedding party or other participants

Finalize any photo shot requests with photographer

Confirm any reservations for wedding weekend

Draft and print wedding program

Get wedding dress steamed, if needed

Finalize rehearsal dinner program

2 to 3 DAYS BEFORE WEDDING

✓ **TASK**

Spa treatments

Attend bridal brunch

Deliver welcome baskets to the hotel, if applicable

Print dinner rehearsal signs or programs

DAY BEFORE THE WEDDING

✓ **TASK**

Get manicure and pedicure

Attend wedding rehearsal

Have fun at rehearsal dinner

Give wedding party and parents gifts

Try to get to bed early

WEDDING DAY

✓ **TASK**

Eat a good breakfast

Give maid of honor wedding announcements to mail, if applicable

Allow yourself plenty of time to get ready

Give wedding rings, officiate fee, and vendor gratuity envelopes to best man

Relax and have fun!

POST WEDDING

✓ **TASK**

Return tuxes and other rentals; get wedding dress to cleaners

Open wedding gifts; send thank you cards

Choose wedding photos for albums (yours and parent's album)

P3 Sample Wedding Budget

Date: October 4, 2014

Time: 6 PM- 1 AM

Total/Working Budget: $25,000			
RECEPTION (50 percent)			
	Budgeted Amount	**Vendor Estimate**	**Actual Spent**
	12,500	12500	
Total	12,500	12500	**750**
Venue and rentals (.25)	3500	3500	750
Food and Service (.55)	7000		
Beverages (.05)	550		
Cake (.10)	1250		
Miscellaneous fees (.05)	200		
ATTIRE (10 percent)			
	2,500	2,500	
Total	2,500	0	0
Gown and alterations (.60)	1500		
Headpiece and veil (.10)	250		
Bridal Accessories (.10)	250		
Hair and makeup (.10)	250		
Groom's tux or suit			
Miscellaneous fees (.10)	250		
FLOWERS AND DECORATIONS (10 percent)			
	2,500	2,500	
Total	2,500	0	0
Floral arrangements-- ceremony (.10)	250		
Flower maid buds/basket (.03)	75		
Ring Pillow	0		
Bride bouquet (.08)	200		
Bridesmaid bouquet (.08)	200		
Boutonnieres (.04)	100		
Corsages (.04)	100		
Reception Decorations (.50)	1250		

Lighting (.13)	325		

MUSIC (10 percent)			
	2,500	2,500	
Total	2,500	0	0
Ceremony Musicians (.10)	250		
Reception band, DJ, entertainment (.50)	1250		
Cocktail-hour musicians (.10)	250		
Sound system or dance floor rental (.15)			
Miscellaneous fees (.15)	250		

PHOTOGRAPHS & VIDEO (10 percent)			
	2500	2500	
Total	2500	0	0
Photography	2500		
Videography	0		
Additional prints and albums	0		
Miscellaneous fees	0		

FAVORS & GIFTS (3 percent)			
	750	750	
Total	750	0	0
Welcome gifts for out of town guests (.65)	500		
Bridesmaids gifts (.20)	150		
Miscellaneous fees (.15)	100		

CEREMONY (2 percent)			
	500	500	
Total	500	0	0
Site fee (.20)	0		
Officiate fee or church donation (.60)	300		
Miscellaneous fees (.20)	200		

STATIONERY (4 percent)			
	1000	1000	
Total	1000	159	121
Save-the-date cards (.20)	200	159	41

Invitations and RSVP's (.50)	500		
Programs (.06)			
Seating and place cards (.06)	60		
Menu cards (.06)	60		
Thank-you notes (.06)	60		
Postage (.06)	60		
Miscellaneous fees (.06)			
WEDDING RINGS (0 percent)			
	0	0	
Total	0	0	0
Bride's ring			
Groom's ring			

Wedding Budget Worksheet

Date: _____

Time: _____

Total/Working Budget: $_____

RECEPTION (50 percent)

	Budgeted Amount	Vendor Estimate	Actual Spent
Total			
Venue and rentals (.25)			
Food and Service (.55)			
Beverages (.05)			
Cake (.10)			
Miscellaneous fees (.05)			

ATTIRE (10 percent)

	Budgeted Amount	Vendor Estimate	Actual Spent
Total		0 .	0
Gown and alterations (.60)			
Headpiece and veil (.10)			
Bridal Accessories (.10)			
Hair and makeup (.10)			
Groom's tux or suit			
Miscellaneous fees (.10)			

FLOWERS AND DECORATIONS (10 percent)

	Budgeted Amount	Vendor Estimate	Actual Spent
Total			
Floral arrangements-- ceremony (.10)			
Flower maid buds/basket (.03)			
Ring Pillow			
Bride bouquet (.08)			
Bridesmaid bouquet (.08)			
Boutonnieres (.04)			
Corsages (.04)			
Reception Decorations (.50)			
Lighting (.13)			

MUSIC (10 percent)

Total
Ceremony Musicians (.10)
Reception band, DJ, entertainment (.50)
Cocktail-hour musicians (.10)
Sound system or dance floor rental (.15)
Miscellaneous fees (.15)

PHOTOGRAPHS & VIDEO (10 percent)

Total
Photography
Videography
Additional prints and albums
Miscellaneous fees

FAVORS & GIFTS (3 percent)

Total		0	0
Welcome gifts for out of town guests (.65)			
Bridesmaids gifts (.20)			
Miscellaneous fees (.15)			

CEREMONY (2 percent)

Total		0	0
Site fee (.20)			
Officiate fee or church donation (.60)			
Miscellaneous fees (.20)			

STATIONERY (4 percent)

Total
Save-the-date cards (.20)
Invitations and RSVP's (.50)
Programs (.06)
Seating and place cards (.06)
Menu cards (.06)
Thank-you notes (.06)
Postage (.06)
Miscellaneous fees (.06)

WEDDING RINGS (0 percent)

Total	0
Bride's ring	
Groom's ring	

TRANSPORTATION (1 percent)

Total	
Limousine or car rental bride/groom (.50)	
Limousine or car rental bridal party (.50)	
Transportation for out of town guests	
Valet parking	
Miscellaneous fees	

TOTALS

Wedding Theme Worksheet

This worksheet will help you begin to think about potential wedding themes. Good luck!

1	*Where did you and your fiancé meet?*
2	*How do you two spend your weekends?*
3	*What are your favorite activities to do together?*
4	*What are your favorite colors? Sports teams? Movies or shows?*
5	*What is your favorite city in the world?*
6	*Did you and your fiancé grow up in the city, a suburb, or a farm?*
7	*How is your relationship unique from your closest friends?*

Venue Evaluation Worksheet

Answer the following questions in the space provided. Then consider potential themes that you could do based on your responses.

What's your ideal size wedding?
Do you and your fiancé share the same faith?
Is it important to either of you to be married in a church?
Do you want to get married in a non-traditional venue such as: • **A garden?** • **Hotel or Reception Hall?** • **Restaurant?** • **Museum?** • **Historical site?** • **On a boat?** • **Industrial space**
Do you want to hold your ceremony and reception at the same location?
What perks are you looking for in a venue? • **Chairs?** • **Tables?** • **Candles?** • **Linens?**
Is the venue well lit?
Does venue have adequate parking?
Will securing the venue get you exclusive use or will you share venue with other brides?
Is the cancellation policy reasonable?

Catering Contract Checklist

A standard catering contract includes the following:

✓	Contract Term
	Address and contact information of all parties including the venue, client information, and caterer information
	Deposit amount
	Cancellation policy
	Final guest count due date
	Fee for child meals, if applicable
	Final payment due date
	Forms of payment accepted
	Number of plates or number of guests to be provided for
	How many servers
	How many bartenders
	Dress code for catering staff
	Food standards (i.e. "no pre-package foods")
	How to handle menu changes in writing
	Maximum price caterer can spend for food (i.e. "market rate")
	Right to reserve catering up to a certain time, in event wedding is cancelled do to an emergency such as fire or flood.
	Any complimentary services provided such as cake cutting
	Set up and break down procedures and any fee
	Time of arrival to venue
	Commitment to view the venue, especially if they have never worked there before
	What items are included in service: linens, flatware, candles, table glasses, bar glasses, etc.
	Certification that caterer holds a current food facility permit, food handler permit, certificate of insurance for the venue and/or state
	Outlines how leftovers will be handled (packaged, donated, etc.)
	Name of catering manager overseeing the event with contact information
	Percentage of food to be prepared over guest counts (i.e. "caterer will provide 10% overage based on final number of guest count registered by client."

Musician Contract Checklist

A standard musician contract includes the following:

✓	Contract Term
	Your name and address and contact information
	Deposit amount
	Payment schedule and final payment due date
	Cancellation policy
	Event type with date, time, and location information
	Address and contact information for reception venue
	Name and phone number of musician performing for your event
	Hours musicians will play as well as when they will perform (specify prelude, ceremony, cocktail hour, and reception)
	Arrival time of musicians to venue
	Type of services being provided
	Fee and overtime rates
	Names of musician who will perform and scheduled time
	Authorization to Contract for event
	Decorum or Code of Conduct (i.e. musician agrees to comply with any venue requires such as volume, language, etc.)
	Dress code for vendor and vendor staff
	Security
	Backup plan detailing who will perform in their place should anyone be delayed or have to cancel;
	Basic outline of duties, including special requests and instructions
	Equipment to be provided by band or DJ
	Number and length of breaks that DJ will take
	Whether meals included
	All fees and overtime rates
	How parties will handle changes to the contract, including unforeseen accidents or emergencies that cause a delay or change to the services or event details

Cake Contract Checklist

A standard baker's contract may include the following:

✓	Contract Term
	Your name, address and contact information
	Reception date and time
	Delivery time
	Number of servings
	Number of tiers, if applicable
	Size and shape of tiers
	Flavor of cake(s)
	Cake design or description (i.e. layer 1 (base) is a lemon cake with raspberry filling covered with fondant and designed with purple and yellow flowers, layer 2 (middle) is…)
	Wedding topper
	Price per serving
	Total charges for cake
	Deposit amount, payment schedule and final payment date
	Cancellation policy
	Final guest count due date
	Final payment due date
	How to handle any changes (i.e. to design, flavors, etc.)

Photographer/Videographer Contract Checklist

A standard photographer or videographer contract may include the following:

✓	Contract Term
	Address and contact information of bride and groom and photographer
	Description of services
	Date, time and location of event
	Name of professional(s) who will be on-site to photograph
	Name of backup, if an emergency
	Guarantee of film backup
	Photographer's attire
	Types of photos to be taken including color and/or black and whites, and the poses to be taken
	Number of rolls of film to be shot
	Date time and hours to be worked
	Time frame for delivery of proofs, prints, and albums
	Who owns the negatives
	Total estimated cost for extra albums, prints and profits
	Total estimated costs and overtime fees
	Exclusive photographer and staff
	Deposit amount and payment schedule
	Cancellation policy
	Photographer Materials (e.g. usually this includes their material, negatives, etc.)
	Copyright and reproduction rights
	Client's use after event
	What happens if the photographer has to cancel (i.e. substitute photographer)
	Overtime rate, if applicable
	Photo credits (must not represent wedding photos as your own)
	How contract modifications are handled
	Outline of photos to be taken and when
	Arrival time of photographer and staff
	Dress code for photographer and staff

Florist Contract Checklist

A standard florist contract may include the following:

✓	Contract Term
	Date, specific time and location of wedding day floral delivery
	Amount and color for each type of flower being used in each bouquet, corsage and arrangement
	Wedding colors
	Acceptable flower substitutes (i.e. no daisies, no pink flowers)
	Number of sizes of flowers for bridal party, ceremony (i.e. altar), cocktail hour, and reception (i.e. table arrangements and centerpieces)
	Decorative items such as garlands, wreathes, pew markers
	Expected condition of flowers (i.e. fresh and in bloom, not wilted)
	Style and color of ribbons, candelabras, vases, and other accessories
	Name and contact information for the person responsible for on site set up on wedding day
	Time of arrival for setup and breakdown, if applicable
	List of items used to hold flowers (i.e. tall vases, short vases, etc.)
	List of any rented items and how/when items can be returned (i.e. will florist pick up from venue the following morning)
	Deposit amount, total cost and payment schedule
	Refund or Cancellation policy

Transportation Contract Checklist

A standard transportation contract may include the following:

✓	Contract Term
	Type of car to be rented
	Expected condition of vehicles on day of service
	Date, time and location of pick up
	Additional options and services available (i.e. runner service)
	Expected length of service
	Number of cars to be used for the day
	Name of driver with contact information
	Proof of a clean driving record
	Address and contact information for bride and groom
	Ceremony and reception addresses
	Total cost and rates
	Driver attire
	Overtime rates
	Cancellation and refund policy

Guest List (Names Only) Worksheet

Below is a template for creating your master guest list.

Bride Guest List	Groom Guest List

Bride Family Guest List	Groom Family Guest List

Invitations Worksheet

Below is a template for tracking your invitations

#	First Name	Last Name	Street	City, State ZIP	Date Sent
2	Bob and Mary	Smith	123 Main Street	NY, NY 10007	7/1/2014
1	Susan	Adams	10 Michigan Avenue	Chicago, IL 60290	7/1/2014

Invitations Worksheet

Below is a template for tracking your invitations

#	First Name	Last Name	Street	City, State ZIP	Date Sent
2	Bob and Mary	Smith	123 Main Street	NY, NY 10007	7/1/2014
1	Susan	Adams	10 Michigan Avenue	Chicago, IL 60290	7/1/2014

Wedding Gift Registry Worksheet

Below is a template for keeping track of the gifts you receive and ensures you get those thank you cards out in time.

Item	Purchaser	Date Received	Thank You Sent	Notes
Pinch Carafe	Bob & Mary Smith	09/15/14	9/20/14	Crate & Barrel

Wedding Gift Registry Worksheet

Below is a template for keeping track of the gifts you receive and ensures you get those thank you cards out in time.

Item	Purchaser	Date Received	Thank You Sent	Notes
Pinch Carafe	Bob & Mary Smith	09/15/14	9/20/14	Crate & Barrel

About the Author

I have been successfully planning events for over 20 years. In addition, I have always been super organized about anything of interest to me. People have asked me for years how I plan and organize the way I do and it truly is something that comes naturally.

Currently, I am a licensed attorney in Washington, DC. However, on the road to becoming an attorney I held a variety of positions that prepared me to write this book. For 10 years I worked in high-end retail managing women's fashion, textiles and lingerie stores. Then I decided to go to Law School as it's always been a dream of mine. While earning my law degree I began working in politics and with non-profit organizations. These organizations gave me a multitude of skills that I cannot even begin to list. To my surprise, my political work also elevated my party planning skills! Specifically, I worked at an organization that held some pretty fabulous parties and I was in charge of pulling it all together with the help of some extremely talented vendors. Some of which took me under their wing and allowed me to watch and learn exactly how they do what they do. It was one of the most fun jobs I ever had. Those experiences were part of the reason I felt comfortable planning my wedding from beginning to end. It also gave me the confidence that I could share helpful tips to brides using this book.

The *P3 Wedding Planner* is filled with how-to guides as well as personal accounts of what I went through while planning my own wedding. But here's the thing—I planned a beautiful wedding from beginning to end but ultimately didn't walk down the aisle. So writing this book and the reason for doing so was two-fold: First, I wanted to impart all the party planning tips that I have learned in the event planning industry. Second, I wanted to share my experience in hopes of arming brides with information that helps them avoid the less than ideal situation I found myself in. Most of the wedding books I read didn't do that. Instead, those books sidestepped some of the real obstacles brides face. This is why this process was both unnerving and amazing at times. I'm sure you can understand why this was a particularly cathartic process for me given the circumstance. Nonetheless, many brides feel stressed or alone in the process just as I did. I truly believe that had I known all the drama that so many of us go through—from dealing with vendors to dealing with the delicate feelings of your nearest and dearest, that I may have had a different outcome. My hope for any bride using the *P3* planner is that the personal accounts included give you the sureness that you can plan a spectacular wedding. And while it may come with a few bumps in the road, planning your wedding is more than do-able and you are not alone. I cannot wait to hear about your stories—the highs, the lows, and all the crazy and fun in between! Who knows, maybe your story will be one that inspires the next bride to keep pushing towards that big reward at the end of that beautiful aisle perfectly planned! I cannot thank you enough for trusting me to help you. Cheers!

www.ingramcontent.com/pod-product-compliance
Lightning Source LLC
Chambersburg PA
CBHW061236270326
41930CB00021B/3479